# THE COMPUTERIZATION
# OF SOCIETY

# THE COMPUTERIZATION
# OF SOCIETY

**A Report to the President of France**

Simon Nora and Alain Minc

The MIT Press
Cambridge, Massachusetts, and
London, England

Second printing, 1980
First English language edition
published by The MIT Press, 1980
Originally published as *L'Informatisation de la société* ©
1978, La Documentation Française, Paris

This book was set in IBM Univers
by Eastern Composition Incorporated
and printed and bound by Halliday Lithograph Corp.
in the United States of America.

**Library of Congress Cataloging in Publication Data**
Nora, Simon.
    The computerization of society.

    Translation of L'informatisation de la societé.
    Includes bibliographical references.
    1. Computers and civilization. 2. Telecommunication
—Social aspects—France. 3. Telecommunication—France
—Data processing. I. Minc, Alain, joint author.
II. Title.
QA76.9.C66N6713        303.4'83        79-25472
ISBN 0-262-14031-4

# CONTENTS

**III**

# INTRODUCTION

The word *télématique*, a French neologism coined by Simon Nora and Alain Minc—or, in its Englished version, *telematics*—may soon spread in our language, as it has, already, in France. Telematics is a term used to describe the growing interconnection between computers and telecommunications. It is similar, thus, to the neologism *compunications*, coined by Anthony Oettinger of Harvard, to describe the merger of computers, telephone, and television into a new kind of digital code, a single yet differentiated system that allows for the transmission of data or interaction between persons or computers "speaking to" computers, through telephone lines, cables, microwave relays, or satellites. Which word will prevail is a matter of linguistic convenience;* what is clear is that the term expresses a new reality, an innovation that has the possibility of transforming society in the way that railroads and electricity did in the nineteenth century.

Behind the term is an instrument and a concept. The instrument is the computer; the concept, information. The computer is not only a computational machine but also a communications device. It can transmit data; it can store and retrieve information; it can be used to simulate complicated reality. It is also, thus, an information device. As Lewis Branscomb has written,

The two terms—information and communication— are often blurred when they are tossed about

---

*Ten years ago, Allan Kiron, a research scientist in the Patent Office, coined the word "domonetics," a word derived from domicile, nexus, and electronics, to indicate the change in living patterns that the decentralization of work would make possible. Others have probably coined similar terms in the past, for the idea has been "in the air" for a long time.

loosely, but it is important to make the distinction if one is to look at what may happen in the upcoming years. Communicating, from an engineering point of view, means simply moving electronic traffic from one place to another. It matters little if the signal represents random noise or a Shakespeare sonnet. When information is available in machine-readable form it can be both processed and communicated. Processing permits meaningful manipulation of the contents of the electronic traffic, thus enhancing its value.*

The comparison between electricity and information made by Nora and Minc in this volume is useful in a different sense. The harnessing of energy was the necessary condition for the creation of an industrial society. The original form of energy was steam power, and the instrument the steam engine. But steam condenses too quickly and loses heat, so machines had to be bunched together near the sources of steam. Electricity is not only a steadier source of power; it permits the enlargement of scale so that machines can be spread far apart, for electricity can be sent hundreds of miles over power lines.

Telecommunications also enlarges scale and permits messages to be sent over large distances. But information differs from electricity in the obvious sense that people *react to* information, and the enlargement of scale ties the entire world together more quickly, and creates more volatile situations, than at any other time in human history.

For the next decade, the means whereby *telematics* or *compunications* are likely to change the patterns of transactions and work can be specified:

1. *Data processing networks* These register pur-

*Lewis Branscomb, "Information: The Ultimate Frontier," *Science*, 12 January 1979, p. 143. (I have rearranged Mr. Branscomb's paragraph to emphasize the relevant point.)

chases in stores through computer terminals into bank transfers. Orders for goods, such as automobiles, can be sent by computer network and registered into programming and scheduling series on the production lines; invoices and inventories are controlled through computer programs. In a broad sense, this is the replacement of much of the "paper economy" by an electronic transfer system.

2. *Information banks and retrieval systems* These recall or search for information through computer memories and print out a legal citation, a chemical abstract, census data, market research material, and the like.

3. *Teletext systems* In these systems, such as the British Post Office's Prestel system (formerly called View Data) or the French Antiope system, news, weather, financial information, classified advertisements, catalogue displays, and research materials can be displayed, through code selection, on home television consoles. What this does, in effect, is to combine the Yellow Pages of the telephone book, the classified advertisements of the newspapers, standard reference materials, and news in a constantly updated fashion, immediately available for consultation.

4. *Facsimile systems* Documents and similar materials (invoices, order, mail) can be sent electronically, rather than by postal transportation systems.

5. *Interactive on-line computer networks* These allow executives or research teams or government agencies to maintain continuous communication so as to translate research results, orders, or financial information into further action.

But telematics (or *télématique*; I prefer the French for the euphony) is, as Nora and Minc in-

sist—and this is one of the virtues of their book—
more than simply the transformation of business
systems or research modes, or even communications. The "computerization of society" will shape,
allow, facilitate, determine—which verb will be the
operative one depends upon our consciousness and
public policy—an extraordinary transformation,
perhaps even greater in its impact than the industrial revolution of the previous century. By en-
larging the scale of communications, it is speeding
a new international division of labor in which capital transfers, market information, and sale and
purchase orders can be transacted on a worldwide
scale, in real time. By the development of terminals, time-sharing, digital networks and the like,
we can, if we choose, decentralize economic activities and reshape life styles and work patterns.
Given the new "horizontal" communication networks that are now possible, the political system
of a country may confront a radically new type of
social structure. And even culture is stridently
affected, from the increasing use of standardized
"processed languages," replacing idiom and collo-
quial speech, to the way in which the blend of picture, sound, and information retrieval can provide
new cultural models.

It is a rare moment in cultural history when we
can self-consciously witness a large-scale social
transformation (as distinct from a revolution). Few
persons realized, when the industrial revolution
was beginning, the import of what was taking
place. The term itself was coined only a hundred
years after the start of the process, by Arnold
Toynbee, in 1884, when he gave a set of lectures
retrospectively viewing the era that he called "The
Industrial Revolution." Today, with our greater

sensitivity to social consequences and to the future—indeed, with a readiness to hail any new gadget (conditioned as we are by science fiction) as the magic wand of social change—we are more alert to the possible imports of technological and organizational change; and this is all to the good, for to the extent that we are that sensitive, we can try and estimate the consequences and decide which policies we should choose, consonant with the values we have, in order to shape, accept, or even reject the alternative futures that are available to us. And that is the singular importance of the Nora/Minc book, for it is one of the first efforts of its kind to make such a wholesale estimate and to pose some crucial questions for society.

*The Computerization of Society*, which was a publishing success and even a best-seller in France after its appearance in January 1978, was written as a report to the President of France. To understand both circumstances, one has to sketch, even if only briefly, some salient aspects of the French political system.

The backbone of the French political system is an elite administrative class, and the basis of its influence is a centralization of administrative power that goes back to Richelieu and Louis XIV. It is this centralized administration that, as Tocqueville emphasized long ago in *The Old Regime and the French Revolution* (see part 2, chapter 2), is responsible for the continuity of the French political system, despite the vicissitudes of revolution, Bonapartism, restoration, republic, war, Pétain, republic, Gaullism, and so on.

Since the end of World War II, this administrative structure has been run by the *Enarchs*, that is the graduates of the Ecole Nationale d'Administration, or ENA, the advanced school for the training of the higher civil servants of France.* The top-ranked graduates of each class (about 10 percent out of one hundred and fifty) are named as *inspecteurs des finances* or as members of the *conseil d'état*. The *conseil d'état* is an appellate and judicial body for all administrative decisions as well as a technical adviser for the drafting of all bills; it goes back in lineage to the former *conseil du roi*. The *inspecteurs des finances* go back to the controller-general, who, as Tocqueville pointed out, "had the whip hand in the conduct of public business and he had gradually brought under his control everything that had to do with money; in other words, almost the entire administration of the country." In France, as in almost all Western countries, fiscal power is effective power; it was always thus, and thus it is today.

But the *inspecteurs des finances* are more than the controllers of the French system. As members of an elite corps, forming an "old-boy network" of

*ENA is one of the *grandes écoles* of France, the special elite schools which are open only by competitive examination and are distinct from the regular university system. Thus the *Ecole Normale Supérieure* was set up in 1808 to train professors; the *Ecole Polytechnique* in 1794, to train engineers. Graduates of the first are called *normaliens* (a distinction they carry through the rest of their lives; such distinguished intellectuals as Henri Bergson, Emile Durkheim, Jean-Paul Sartre, and Raymond Aron are *normaliens*); graduates of the second are called *polytechniciens*. Though the career lines are no longer so exact— one can become a university professor without being *normalien* or *agrégé* (i.e., taking the special examination that serves as a screening device)—selection to these schools still functions as a way to mark the "coming men" of French intellectual and technocratic life. However, membership in the higher civil service comes only through ENA.

friends and rivals, they become the advisers to
politicians, they are recruited for the lucrative administrative posts in French industry and finance,
and sometimes they even become politicians themselves. Valéry Giscard d'Estaing, the President of
France, was an *inspecteur des finances.* So, too,
was Simon Nora, who was a member of the first
class, of 1947—though their political paths often
diverged.*

One of the tasks that *inspecteurs des finances* are
called upon to do is to write the major reports that
assess public enterprises and public policy issues
in France; these reports serve as the basis for the
renovation of old policies or the adoption of new
ones.** In December 1976, Giscard d'Estaing
asked Nora to do a survey of the impacts of computers and the new communications technology
on French society, and in January 1978, working
with Alain Minc, a younger *inspecteur des finances*,
and a team of specialists, Nora submitted the report, which was published as *L'informatisation de
la société* by the French government printing office, La Documentation Française. The major docu-

*Nora, born in 1921, was active in the French Resistance,
serving in the Maquis group of Vercors. After graduation
from ENA in 1947, Nora was a member of the team that
first set up the French system of National Economic Ac-
counts. In 1955–56, he was a member of the cabinet of
Pierre Mendès-France. He was director of the European
Coal and Steel Community, an adviser to Prime Minister
Chaban-Delmas in 1969-1971, and from 1971 to 1974
the *directeur-général* (or chief operating executive) of
Hachette, the second largest publishing house (after Time-
Life) in the world and the largest in France and Europe.
In 1974, Nora returned to the Ministry of Finance, where
he was given the top rank of *inspecteur-général*.
**Nora, for example, was responsible for such major reports
as the survey of public enterprises for Pompidou and, before the one on Télématique, on the renovation of the
central cities of France.

ment was an overview of the situation; with it were four supplementary volumes, whose contents are summarized at the conclusion of the report.*

The Nora/Minc report became the source of an instantaneous and widespread public discussion (and was published commercially in the popular series Dix-Dix Huit) for two reasons. One was the intrinsic fascination of the subject matter—and its large rhetorical scope, almost an eschatological fantasy—which had not been covered before by the French press. Thus, it has the impact of a modern Jules Verne story. Second, was the fact that France has been going through an intensive period of self-scrutiny in which the traditional centralization of administrative power was increasingly under question (Paris elected its first self-governing administrative body and its first mayor in 1977), and the Nora/Minc report raised quite directly the possibility of reorganizing the political structure and the decentralizing of society as a result of *télématique*. (There was also—and this should not be minimized—the impact a new concept or new idea can have when it is expressed in a bold new word.)

For an American reader, much of the discussion of the character of the computer and telecommunications will not be new, though their salient effects are often summarized beautifully by the two authors.** What is most interesting to an Ameri-

---

*The four supplementary volumes are "Nouvelle informatique et nouvelle croissance," containing six appendixes or background papers; "Industrie et services informatiques," with three appendixes; "La nouvelle informatique et ses utilisateurs," with three appendixes and a bibliography; and a fourth volume, "Documents contributifs," with ten special papers.

**For further discussion, see Michael L. Dertouzos and Joel Moses, eds., *The Computer Age: A Twenty-Year View* (Cambridge, Mass.: The MIT Press, 1979).

can reader is that the Nora/Minc book becomes a "looking-glass" reflecting French society as it confronts a major technological-sociological challenge. The importance of the Nora/Minc report is that it calls for and prescribes a unified national policy to utilize the new technology of *télématique.*

France is a *"société bloquée"*—a term of Stanley Hoffmann's used in France as the title of a book by the French sociologist Michel Crozier—a point of view implicitly endorsed by Nora and Minc. It is a society that has become increasingly rigidified in its bureaucratic and political institutions, and thereby less able to respond readily to the shocks of change that engulf it. The Nora/Minc report seeks to show how a new technology can reshape a social structure and why the political system has to change to meet the new scales of economic life and the new patterns of social life that result.

To an American reader, however, there may be another surprise: a cultural shock at the tone of urgency regarding the role of US domination in computers, in satellite systems, and in telecommunications, and the need to meet that challenge. Few Americans, absorbed almost provincially in their own troubles, are aware of the image of America held by other countries, particularly by France. For France, the American domination of telecommunications and computers is a threat to its independence—in the crucially significant if not overriding area of technology and in the field of culture, where the American presence, through television and satellite, becomes an omnipresence.

Whether this perception is accurate, and whether the threat is actual—the tone of the Nora/Minc report recalls the earlier alarm voiced by Jacques Servan-Schreiber, in his *Le Défi Americain*, which

warned, in 1967, of the overwhelming lead of the
United States in high technology, a lead that seems
to have evaporated in this decade—is a question
that is subject to debate. Yet the fact that these
feelings are held by responsible French officials is
palpable, and important for American understanding.

In a broader political and sociological sense, the
Nora/Minc report raises a different question for
the United States. In this volume, two astute ob-
servers, aided by a team of technical specialists,
have surveyed a major technological and social
innovation and have proposed a unified national
policy to deal with the impending changes. In the
United States where the scale of activities in this
field is considerably larger than in France, there is
as yet no national policy.

We are now on the threshold of a major set of
developments which, with the energy problem,
will once again reshape our lives. A quiet debate has
been taking place in the United States, obscured
largely by the energy issue. There are before the
96th Congress three bills to modify the Communications Act of 1939. If passed, these would open
up the telecommunications field to more competition and give the market a more important voice
in shaping the development of "compunications."
To that extent, the direction of the United States
is opposed to that of France, where the effort—if
the Nora/Minc report is implemented—will be to
give the government a more active role in the
introduction of *télématique*. It is for this reason
as well—for the contrast in policy it provides—that
the Nora/Minc report is of interest to us.

Daniel Bell
June 1979

Paris
December 20, 1976

**The President of the Republic**

To:
Mr. Simon Nora
Inspector Général des Finances
93, rue de Rivoli
75001 Paris

Dear Mr. Nora:
The applications of the computer have developed
to such an extent that the economic and social
organization of our society and our way of life
may well be transformed as a result. Our society
should therefore be in a position both to foster
this development and to control it so that it can
be made to serve the cause of democracy and
human growth.

During the closed session of the Council of
Ministers on April 22, 1975, the decision was
made to appoint an official to head a commission
that would propose suitable guidelines to the
government in this area.

I am aware of your concern with these issues and
would therefore like to entrust you with an
exploratory mission whose aim is twofold: to
stimulate thinking on how the computerization of
society should be carried out and to work out
more precisely the scope of the study and the
nature of the task such a commission should
undertake.

Consequently, I would like to ask you to submit
a report to me on this subject in the coming
months. In your preparation of this report, you
will, of course, be assisted by the departments

concerned, particularly those coming under the
authority of the minister of industry and research;
the ministry of economics and finance will also
provide you with the necessary material and
administrative support.

Sincerely,
Valéry Giscard d'Estaing

**Inspection Générale des Finances**

Dear Mr. President:

I have been entrusted by you with an exploratory mission aimed at "stimulating thinking on how the computerization of society should be carried out."

Man has long tried to evaluate the effects of technological revolutions on society, but to make such an attempt in the area of the computer, especially with a view toward a possible course of action, means that there must be room for specific proposals.

The topics selected for this report are a function of its purpose, namely, to provide government with the capacity to weigh recommended courses of action and to create, subject to their approval, the means for implementing the chosen course. The report is also aimed at drawing attention to the new obligations imposed upon sociological analysis by technological change.

Any thought that is given to the computer and society reinforces the conviction that the stability of modern civilization depends on a mixture difficult to achieve, i.e., blending the increasingly powerful assertion of the prerogatives of the state (even if they are more strictly confined) with the growing impatience with restraint that characterizes modern society. For better or for worse, information processing will be one of the major ingredients of this mixture.

Alain Minc, inspector of finance, has added his name to mine on this report and has been associated with its planning and preparation to the fullest extent. We assume joint responsibility for its content. So that the report could be issued in due time, our consultations with experts had to be limited, but our conclusions, to be useful, had to be based on authoritative opinion. This function is fulfilled by the eleven appendixes and ten supporting documents. While we assume responsibility for the appendixes, responsibility for the supporting documents is that of their authors alone.

This was the only suitable method in a context where it was as important to determine the scope of the subject as to explore it. Its value lies in the fact that the individual authors were free to express candid, contradictory, and unorthodox opinions that would doubtless have been stifled within the framework of a formal commission. The method's drawback is that the survey is based on voluntary cooperation and as such does not explore topics that failed to evoke interest or that could not be raised owing to insufficient time.

Not all of our recommendations are operational. Some stress the gaps in our knowledge and suggest ways of overcoming them. Others define the short- and medium-term effects of computerization and suggest measures to shape them to fit collective interests. Still others pose questions that can reasonably be used to speculate about our long-range future.

Our conclusions, if they are approved, may be implemented in two ways. One is the rapid establishment of permanent agencies to apply the policy determined by the government. The second is to set up study groups to examine empirically the problems this report does not cover. We suggest that both of these methods be employed simultaneously.

Respectfully yours,
Simon Nora

# THE COMPUTERIZATION
# OF SOCIETY

# 1

## COMPUTERIZATION: A KEY ISSUE IN THE FRENCH CRISIS

If France does not respond effectively to the serious new challenges she faces, her internal tensions will deprive her of the ability to control her fate.

The increasing computerization of society is a key issue in this crisis and could either worsen it or help solve it. Depending on the policy into which it is incorporated, computerization will bring about changes for the better or for the worse; there is nothing automatic or preordained about its effects, which will depend on how relations between the government and French society develop in the coming years.

The clearest and most pressing problems originate from the enormous and brutal increase in the price of imported fuel, affecting our economic and social stability. The task of the next few years is to resolve these problems.

Reactions to this development, however, would be unrealistic if they did not take into account a deeper break with the past, predating the Yom Kippur War, which the well-meaning have termed a crisis of civilization. This crisis is the result of the conflict between traditional values and upheavals caused by industrialization and urbanization: the stage has been set for a long struggle between elitism and democracy, which is ultimately a struggle between knowledge and tradition. The crisis of civilization will outlive the immediate crisis, but the two are closely linked, and it is futile to try to resolve the second by means other than those that will help to resolve the first.

In the short range, France must deal in a coherent way with threats to her economic stability, the "social consensus," and national independence. In effect, the well-being and sovereignty of every industrial nation depends on a stable foreign exchange, a satisfactory level of employment, and its citizens' willingness to play by the rules of the social game. A time-honored bond links these three objectives. What is new is that today their natural harmony has been lost. What were formerly three complementary ambitions have now become opposing forces demanding simultaneous fulfillment, yet the solution required for each one separately calls for a course of action that sets it against the other two.

The appropriate policy must meet three conditions. First, the increase in competitiveness, matched with an industrial policy adapted to the new international division of labor, must generate an increase in markets. The restoration of foreign financing will make it possible to stimulate new domestic demand, thus increasing employment. Financing could then come from the excess in productivity.

Second, the overall organization of society (relations between the state administration and business, between the administration and the citizen, competition between large and small businesses, methods of managing and organizing labor, etc.) must be such that the strain and discipline that accompany the pursuit of development are made acceptable.

Third, this change in economic and social structure can only be brought about if France can avoid excessive pressure from foreign governments or groups whose objectives may run counter to hers. Success may strengthen national independence, but it cannot be compromised at the start if it is to work.

The choice of means for resolving the current crisis cannot ignore the long-term movement affecting French society, which is conveyed by two strong and frequently contradictory aspirations: a wish for emancipation and a hunger for equality, both of which require a reordering of the traditional hierarchies.

None of this can be taken for granted in a country shaped by centuries of centralization, publicly criticized and secretly craved. Society will not recover its powers by anarchically demanding the settlement of its disputes. Nor would it be realistic to think that its powers will be restored merely through the will of the government.

Each technological revolution in the past has brought about far-reaching economic and social reorganization. A technological revolution may simultaneously create a crisis and the means of overcoming it, as was the case with the coming of the steam engine, the railroads, and electricity.

The "computer revolution" will have wider consequences. The computer is not the only technological innovation of recent years, but it does constitute the common factor that speeds the development of all the others. Above all, insofar as it is responsible for an upheaval in the processing and storage of data, it will alter the entire nervous system of social organization.

Until fairly recently, data processing was expensive, unreliable, and esoteric, restricted to a limited number of businesses and operations. Data processing was elitist, a prerogative of the great and powerful. Henceforth, mass computerization will take hold, becoming as indispensable to society as electricity. This transformation can be traced to two technological advances. In the past, the only computers to be found were gigantic. Nowadays, a multitude of small, powerful, and inexpensive machines are on the market. They are no longer isolated from one another, but rather linked together in "networks."

This increasing interconnection between computers and telecommunications — which we will term "telematics" [1] — opens radically new horizons. Means of communication have certainly not been structuring communities only in our own day. Roads, railways, and electricity are so many stages along the way from the family to local, national, and multinational organization.

Unlike electricity, "telematics" will not transmit an inert current, but will convey information, i.e., power. The telephone line or the television channel are the building blocks for this change. Today, they are combined into polyvalent transmitters and are starting to link computers and data banks. Satellites will soon provide them with a potent tool. Telematics will not only be an additional network but a different one as well, blending pictures, sounds, and memories and transforming the pattern of our culture.

In varying degrees, telematics will affect all of the long- and short-term aspects of the French crisis. It will affect the economic balance, modify power relationships, and increase the stakes of sovereignty.

It will bring with it a substantial increase in productivity, which in the beginning will also increase unemployment, particularly in the public service sector. On the other hand, once this productivity has been properly channeled, it will improve our ability to compete and open new markets. It will in this way facilitate the return to an external equilibrium, which is the precondition of growth. The contradiction between the immediate dangers of unemployment and the odds for a subsequent increase in employment can be eliminated only with very strong incentives, stimulating new demand. Determining the mix, and especially the timing of this double policy, consolidating hyper-competitive sectors and generating, through trans-fers, an increase in amenities and collective con-sumption, is a tricky matter. Any slip or excessive lead of one over the other would run up against the traditional obstacles: foreign trade deficits or intolerable rates of unemployment. While the new computerization eases the way for a new type of growth, it presupposes control over it as well.

Telematics offers varied solutions which can be adapted to all forms of control or regulation. It allows the decentralization or even the autonomy of basic units. Better still, it facilitates this decen-tralization by providing peripheral or isolated units with data from which heretofore only huge, centralized entities could benefit. Its task is to simplify administrative structures by increasing their effectiveness and improving their relations with those under their jurisdiction. It also allows the local municipalities more freedom. It reinforces the competitiveness of the small and mid-size busi-ness vis-à-vis the large enterprises. Telematics finds itself at the heart of the power game through the movement it generates in information networks. It shifts the balance between rival markets and among municipalities. It influences certain pro-fessions by modifying their social status. It in-creases contact between social groups and the vulnerability of large organizations.

It would, however, be unrealistic to expect com-puterization alone to overturn the social structure and the hierarchy of power that governs it. The traditions and the cultural model we have inherited from our history favor centralization and administrative proliferation, hierarchic rigidity in big business, and the domination of small business by big business. Our traditions stand in the way of the initiative and adaptability required by a society based on communication and participation.

Only a deliberate policy of social change can both solve the problems raised by telematics and utilize its potential. Such a policy implies a strategy based on the balance of powers and counter-powers and on the capacity of the government to favor development rather than impose it. Telematics can facilitate the coming of a new society, but it cannot construct it on its own initiative.

Telematics also changes the stakes of sovereignty. The first large French computers were the result of a desire for military independence. Seeking autonomy, the public powers have gone on promoting the computer industry. This approach, while it remains partially justified, has become quite inadequate. Today, the game is no longer played exclusively in that arena.

It has to take into account the renewal of the IBM challenge. Once a manufacturer of machines, soon to become a telecommunications administrator, IBM is following a strategy that will enable it to set up a communications network and to control it. When it does, it will encroach upon a traditional sphere of government power, communications. In the absence of a suitable policy, alliances will develop that involve the administrator of the network and the American data banks, to which it will facilitate access.

Only action by the authorities, standardizing the networks, launching communication satellites, and

creating data banks, can give an original model
for society with room to develop.

Widening its ambitions, computerization policy
must begin increasing its strong points now, but
above all it must diversify its handling of them.

The policy must enhance the positive effects of
telematics on productivity and compensate for its
negative effects on employment; it must derive
maximum benefit from newly created possibilities
for reorganizing administration, support small and
medium-size businesses, restructure big business,
and regulate working conditions. Care must be
taken to prevent any portion of the computer industry from dominating any other part and to prevent the industry as a whole from dominating business and the citizenry.

The state cannot be the only entity to promote
such a policy, however, and cannot be allowed to
adopt an all-or-nothing position.

In some cases, to improve France's position in a
contest with competitors not under her sovereignty, the authorities must make unrestrained use of
their trump card, which is to decree. In others, because participants on the national scale are of unequal strength, the authorities must support the
weaker parties by regulating. In still others, and
these are the most common cases, the need is to
increase the autonomy and responsibility of forces
that in trying to assert themselves run into obstacles, primary among them the government itself. Here the authorities must encourage opposition and take it upon themselves to withdraw.
This choice between decree, regulation, and with-
drawal is not arbitrary; it expresses an overall conception of society.

The only "cartel" capable of establishing a dialogue with IBM is one that could be formed from

an alliance of telecommunications agencies. The
basic task of the authorities, then, is to strengthen
the French role in this association. By acting as a
lever in this way, they will realize the objectives
and means for establishing a national communications policy. This requires both a more concentra-
ed administration and a more active set of administrators. A Ministry of Communications must
be created for coordinating the DGT (Direction
Générale des Télécommunications — General Telecommunications Administration), TDF (Télé-
Diffusion de France — French Broadcasting), and
CNES (Centre National des Etudes Spatiales — National Center for Space Studies).

The DGT itself must be adapted to an expanding
market, and must acquire greater mobility. To do
so would require the separation of the postal and
telecommunications services, and for the latter,
the creation of a national company that would
allow it the required degree of flexibility. A more
autonomous role will allow these agencies to
exercise more control.

Government policy toward the other participants
in the computer game must be both eclectic and
pragmatic, taking the strengths and weaknesses of
each into account. It must support the companies
that provide computer-related services, a sector
that is dynamic but fragmented; it must allow
powerful public intervention in the field of research, provide incentives linked to the activities
of the manufacturers for the component parts of
the computer industry, and finally, once its
strategy has been determined, it must allot a proper role to the national manufacturer of large
computers.

In France, perhaps more than anywhere else, the
administration is a driving force and serves as an

example. Unknown to the authorities, the development of telecommunications systems can bring its organization to a standstill for decades. It must endow itself with the means to predict this and control it. A General Delegation for Administrative Reform under the prime minister could explore possible developments and offer guidelines. If this delegation were established, it would not be a center of power in the administrative hierarchy but a tool for supervision, planning, and promotion. Its objective would be to make use of telematics to prepare for useful rationalizations of industry, and above all to expedite decentralization and the lightening of the administrative burden.

Authorities will develop tools to make their policy work by acting with strength where power relationships dominate the scene, and by restricting their actions and decentralizing when the needed changes require other groups to take the initiative.

If the government can perceive and correct in time the imbalances that computerization can aggravate, and the restrictions and constraints it may generate, it may realize the necessary changes within the next ten years without setting off the "inflexibility/explosion" sequence familiar to our country. These stakes are vital, but they are limited as well. Even if these policies meet with reasonable success, their only merit will be to set the stage for the real upheaval of civilization for which the computer revolution may be responsible over the long term.

Anxiety makes people long for a rational, certain future. It increases when profound changes uproot traditional values. For a hundred years now, the most spectacular transformations of society have had technological bases, which makes it tempting to predict a future controlled by technology itself. At present this vision is represented by telematics and finds expression in contradictory illusions.

The pessimists emphasize the risks involved — rising unemployment, social rigidity, the vulgarization of life. They see computerization as a victory for the impersonal, repetitive nature of tasks and the elimination of jobs. It would solidify the unwieldiness and the hierarchical nature of organizations, reinforcing the omniscience of those "in the know" while automatizing the others. All that would remain would be the computerizers and the computerized, the users and the used. The machine would no longer be a computer (*ordinateur*), a tool for calculating, remembering, and communicating, but a mysterious and anonymous order-giver (*ordonnateur*). Society would become opaque, to itself and to its individual members, but at the same time dangerously transparent, to the detriment of freedom, to those possessed of the demiurgic technology and their masters.

On the other hand, the optimists believe that miracles are within reach, that computerization means information, information means culture, and culture means emancipation and democracy. Anything that increases access to information facilitates dialogue on a more flexible and personal level, encourages increased participation and more individual responsibilities, and strengthens the ability of the weak and the "little man" to resist the encroachments of the Leviathan, the economic and social powers-that-be.

This dream and this nightmare at least share the same questions. Are we headed, regardless of appearances and alibis, toward a society that will use this new technology to reinforce the mechanisms of rigidity, authority, and domination? Or, on the other hand, will we know how to enhance adapt-ability, freedom, and communication in such a way that every citizen and every group can be re-sponsible for itself?

In fact, no technology, however innovative it may be, has long-term fatal consequences. The development of society determines its effects rather than being constrained by them. It so hap-pens that in the years to come the primary chal-lenge will no longer involve the ability of the more advanced human societies to control nature. This has already been acquired. The challenge instead lies in the difficulty of building the system of con-nections that will allow information and social organization to progress together. Under certain conditions, computerization can facilitate this development.

Thus, the headspinning computerization evokes is beside the point, not because it is ephemeral but because it is being transformed into the question of the future of society itself: will a civilization based on high productivity be calm and un-emotional or will it remain in conflict? Will the groups in opposition be structured as they are to-day by their role in the process of production and their ability to consume, or will we gradually see a dismantling of tradition, with individuals identify-ing themselves with a multiplicity of groups striv-ing to dominate specific elements of the cultural model?

The traditional tools for interpreting society and forecasting its future would not be much help in such a case. If they cannot even accurately predict the outcome of struggles tied to production, they certainly cannot describe a world progressively escaping from it. The new challenge is one of uncertainty: there can be no accurate forecasts, only good questions on the means to advance toward the desired goal. The future can no longer be determined by prediction, but rather through planning and the capacity of each country to organize itself in order to achieve it.

The authorities will no longer be able to call upon the old methods and objectives, which are almost certain to fail. Preparation for the future implies inculcating a freedom that will cause even the most deep-rooted habits and ideologies to lose their validity. This requires an adult society that can enhance spontaneity, mobility, and imagination while accepting the responsibilities of total regulation; it also requires a government that — while openly exercising its prerogatives — acknowledges that it can no longer be the only star of the social drama.

# 2 FROM DATA PROCESSING TO TELEMATICS

We are in a computer boom. Countless small, efficient, and inexpensive machines are appearing on the market. They could be the harbingers of freedom. A technology for the elite has given way to a way of life for the masses.

Simultaneously, telematics is springing to life, born of the marriage between computers and communication networks, which will culminate in the arrival of universal satellites, transmitting images, data, and sounds.

## The Information Explosion

After progressing continuously and rapidly for two decades, data processing today is undergoing accelerated change. Manufacturers have not stopped improving their computers, diversifying them, and increasing their level of performance, but this has not changed the type of equipment offered the users nor the method by which data processing has been incorporated into large organizations.

For some years now, extraordinary changes in electronic components,* along with a few other spectacular advances, have been broadening the computerization field to an almost unlimited extent. Increasingly smaller, inexpensive, yet reliable machines are available on the market.

At the same time, computer networks have begun to infiltrate business, decentralizing the collection of data, allowing employees as a whole access, in real time,* to files and processing capabilities. It is at this point that the differences disappear between large and small machines, between access terminals and processing centers,* while the seemingly natural boundary between hardware and software* begins to fade away.

*Terms marked by an asterisk may be found in the glossary.

The Past: Data
Processing for the
Elite[1]

The history of data processing has been identified
with a series of technical innovations; up until now,
however, generations of equipment followed one
another in succession without basically modifying
the user's relation to it.

The computers of the fifties were still complex
and hard to handle. They used transistors* and
were bulky (several cubic meters in size) and
fragile. When they broke down, their size and cir-
cuitry meant frequent and difficult repairs. In addition, these early computers were accessible only
in machine language,* later in assemblers* —
only a few data technicians trained to conduct an
esoteric dialogue were capable of understanding it.
General use was handicapped by the clumsy rules
governing management of the computer. Furthermore, all of these different materials were incompatible,* meaning that a program could not be
transferred from one machine to another.

Complex and difficult to operate, the early computers were restricted in use and tedious, truly
machines for "the unhappy few."

This initial period, which recent advances would
liken to the prehistoric age of data processing,
ended in 1965 with the generation of IBM 360
computers. The first integrated circuits* replaced
transistors, allowing for a significant improvement
in the performance/price ratio, at the same time
decreasing the size of the machines and increasing
their reliability. This new equipment constituted a
universal line of products, capable of carrying out
management tasks as well as scientific calculations.
Moreover, they were compatible,* which made it
possible for the user to switch from one machine
to another without rewriting all of his programs,
provided machines from the same manufacturer
were used. And the language became simpler.

"COBOL," "FORTRAN," and "PL 1" were all programming languages requiring only a short period of initiation. These advances facilitated the use of data processing. The user became less obsessed with the operation of the computer itself and could thereby escape from the traditional data-processing applications (payroll, money orders) and devote himself freely to analyzing other tasks to be computerized.

This development was not equated with a metamorphosis of data processing. Certain technical restrictions remained: sequential access[*] to the files prevented the user from finding what he wanted directly. In addition, the batch-processing[*] method, which was still the rule, forced him to relinquish data, with the time needed to punch them in, enter them into the machine, and recover the results.

At this stage, data processing enjoyed a special status within the large corporations: isolated, because it depended on machines all located in the same place, centralized, since it brought back all of the data from the user services, and even traumatic, because it delivered a finished product after an operation that resembled alchemy. Data processing at this stage in its development was reserved for a minority of businesses which could afford the high investment in men and equipment. In France, 250 businesses had 80 percent of the total number of computers in service in 1970.

Of course, smaller computers began to appear, ones that were less reliable and less expensive but that still had all of the traditional features of this initial stage of computerization. There was only one form of data processing; thus there was only one type of customer and only one type of data processor.

A Ray of Progress

Of all the recent advances, the development of electronic components is without doubt the one most fraught with consequences. Their almost inconceivable miniaturization and ridiculously low cost are practically equivalent to an alteration in nature. Nowadays, a microprocessor* only a few millimeters wide contains the same processing capability as a computer which ten or fifteen years ago was the epitome of technological achievement and took up an entire room. If a component cost 350 francs ten years ago, its equivalent can now be produced for one centime. If the price of a Rolls Royce had evolved in comparable fashion, the most luxurious model would cost one franc today.

The consequences are every bit as significant as the change. It is now possible to manufacture small, powerful, and inexpensive computers accessible to the average user. This has been accompanied by a reduction in the cost of the central units* of standard computers, the manufacturing price of which has decreased a thousand times in ten years. The manufacturers can now focus their efforts on other elements of the data-processing system, particularly on increasingly accessible and clearer languages. Advances such as these effectively transform their policies. They are no longer obliged to fight for a scrap of power here, a scrap there. They now have the freedom to improve the reliability of the instrument and distribute its processing power over several points of the system.

It has also become possible to incorporate part of the basic software* into the components themselves. Manufacturers can now offer the user more effective equipment. It also gives them the opportunity to "lock in" their customers, by making it more difficult to change suppliers.

At the same time, the restrictions inherent in the previous generation are breaking down one after another. Data that were once available only sequentially can now be obtained directly with the use of special procedures. Data banks are part of the logic of this progress, linking the advantage of a fantastic storage capability with facilities for easy access.[2]

In addition, the data-handling system* is becoming more flexible. The machine manages its own operation with increasing effectiveness, optimizing the work sequences and organizing in the best possible way the processing, data acquisition, and printing times.

The access languages are also coming increasingly to resemble lingua franca. The rigid semantics of COBOL and the assembler in particular are becoming a thing of the past, while the outlook for programming in an everyday or quasi-everyday language is now within the realm of possibility.

One major phenomenon is the appearance of systems in real time.* The central unit and the files are located within a complex system having more numerous access points and in which an increasing number of terminals can communicate with each other and with computers.

Although taken up separately for purposes of analysis, these advances are linked together in the marketing strategy of each of the manufacturers. In a market where competition is particularly keen and where every innovation is the result of a massive research effort, each new step taken by an industrialist forces all of the others to follow or to drop out of the game. This gives rise to a headstrong policy to force the customers to remain faithful to their supplier. Faced with the development of microprocessors, then, obliging the manu-

facturers of components to become data-processing professionals, the traditional producers are
offering their customers increasingly elaborate
services, such as data banks and systems architectures.*

The Future: Data       These innovations make it possible to offer the
Processing for the     most widely varying products to increasingly
Masses                 numerous users. The machine will become a part
                       of our daily lives.

The users are offered an extraordinarily diversified choice and, based on their objectives and constraints, must seek out the arrangement that best
suits them. This may be either in the form of a
single large computer or a veritable erector set of
smaller ones.

Some manufacturers offer machines with neither
software nor maintenance, mostly either producers
of components who have increased their scope of
activities or "snipers" who have intentionally
placed themselves on the fringes of the IBM empire
in an attempt to produce a certain piece of equipment identical to IBM's at a lower cost, but without providing any service. Other manufacturers
limit themselves to producing computers and their
accompanying software without incorporating
them into complex networks. Still others, the
oldest and largest, offer "telematic" systems with
multiple central units, ponderous data banks, and
a suitable number of terminals which are in addition adaptable and expandable.

The possibility of meeting the needs of a large
number of users at affordable prices makes the
universe of the computer almost limitless. Instead
of remaining the prerogative of a few large, powerful firms, it is opening up its doors to hundreds of

thousands of potential users, to small and mid-size businesses, the professions, and even homes, whose capacity for dialogue, demands, and financial resources call for a diversified approach.

Data processing is leaving its ghetto behind. Relations between the user and the machine are losing their "demiurgic" aspect. Henceforth, a brief period of apprenticeship will enable any employee to use a small computer or an "intelligent terminal."* The personnel of a small business will have access to the calculator and will be able to see its products; indeed, they will be in close contact with the computer department and thus will not feel threatened. In large organizations, as the new systems are gradually installed, they too are moving closer to the work place — the employee or worker himself enters the data, receives the replies in clear language, and makes use of the results.

The increasing cooperation between the computer or the terminal and the user is independent of organizational models, which may differ greatly among themselves. It is the expression of the new data processing, which exists because there is now a network that makes it possible.

**The Transformation of Telecommunications**

Prevoiusly separated means of communication are now converging together on data processing, creating a whole new range of services.

The Past: Separate Worlds

Up until now, television networks and telecommunications networks were clearly differentiated.

Designed like a star, with a single point of emission, the television network is unidirectional, broadcasting from the center toward all of the receivers. On the other hand, telecommunications networks handle the traffic between two points, a transmitter and a receiver; furthermore, the communication can occur in each direction, while the television receiver is condemned to remain totally voiceless.

These technical differences have naturally been accompanied by a division of services, one group aimed at two-directional exchanges and the other at passive information systems.

Until now, data processing was, of course, closer to telecommunications. Requiring connections in both directions between several processing centers or between one processing center and several peripheral terminals, and limited to private information, data processing made do with telephone lines, which guaranteed both availability and secrecy.

This is how the first networks were developed. Those carrying limited amounts of information used normal telephone lines; those requiring larger transmission capacities leased special lines to which they had exclusive rights.

The Increase in
Overlapping Networks

The convergence of means of communication is based on the disappearing difference between one-directional and two-directional networks, on the development of data networks, and on the increasing digitalization of signals.[3]

Radio-television networks no longer function exclusively in one direction. They give the receiver some capacity to "send" to the transmitter, certainly more restricted than in the direction of the broadcast but nonetheless sufficient for establishing a dialogue: this response potential may be the result of a coupling with the telephone line. Similarly, the installation of communal television antennae,* provided adequate equipment is added, makes it

possible to join transmission on a more modest
scale with reception. This unequal dialogue is not
a handicap for teleprocessing, in which transmission
is always asymmetrical: one of the two interlocu-
tors briefly orders a processing operation which
the other carries out and whose results, however
enormous, reach him on the large output line.
Transmissions such as these, therefore, can find a
place in the "troughs" of a television network, as
they have heretofore done on telephone lines
alone.

Along with telephone networks, data networks
are also being developed today. The increase in
this traffic (which in 1985 should represent 10
percent of all messages, as opposed to 5 percent
now), the accessibility of data processing to new
ranks of users, and the need to offer more varied
transmission capabilities than those offered by
telephone lines are responsible for this evolution.
From one country to the next, the technological
choices have varied, from circuit switching to
packet switching,[4] but they have all offered features that until now have been specific to the
telephone network, switching and concentration.
Initially designed for data alone, these networks
are now capable of conveying types of messages
customarily reserved for telephone lines or new
types of services, such as telecopying.[5]

This increasingly pronounced overlapping, which
is likely to evolve into substitution, will be facilitated by the gradual disappearance of the separation between digital and analog transmissions.*

Today, the telephone conveys analog signals,
but in the future it will be based on digital signals.
Among other things, this means that dial phones
will have to be speedily replaced by touch-tone
phones.

Television is now analog but can already be transmitted digitally, as can radio: the processes are still in the experimental stage but will probably come into general use within the next ten years. What will be the difference then between computer data, a television picture, a radio sound, or snatches of a phone conversation? Intensity, frequency, output: nothing is more tenuous or less discernible.

Expanding Services

These technical changes bring with them an increase in the services offered to users, whether administrative agencies, businesses, or private parties.[6] Of course, given systems that are frequently limited to a few prototypes, the demand remains unknown. No one can presume to know the outcome of the confrontation between supply and demand, but the field is wide open.

As an example, remote publishing of newspapers in decentralized print shops, which is being done even now, will become widespread; it could easily be accomplished over special phone lines or television channels, as is the case today, or even over data transmission networks. The choice of a support vehicle will depend less on technique than on cost. In the long run, its true competitor will be home publishing of newspapers by the readers themselves. The newspaper will be taken from a telecopier or will appear on the television screen; in the former case, the transmission will be by telephone line, in the latter by a television channel.

In another example, individuals will have access to data banks by telephone and receive replies over their television screens. Systems such as these will also be used for message services, competing with postal or telephone transmission. The user will also be able to select a particular page of the news broadcast over television, using a special instrument for this purpose.[7]

Finally, the spread of the telecopier will go hand in hand with the increase in transfers of digital signals. What could be easier than transmitting a letter over a data network?

Listing the technical possibilities of future services in this way is not done for the joy of compiling lists. It shows the wide potential applications of teleprocessing: at low output, it closely resembles telecopying; at medium output, it is barely distinguishable from consulting a data bank; at high output, it can be likened to remote publishing or even television.

This increasing generalization of the "signal" will reach its peak with the development of transmission satellites.

**The "Telematic" Future: Universal Satellites**

The ease with which communications can be handled by satellite will accelerate the change in data processing. By increasing data transmissions and the exchange of processing operations from country to country and continent to continent, satellites will be responsible for the gradual creation of a worldwide "telematics" networks.

A Privileged Communications Tool

The advantages of power, universality, accessibility, and scope that satellites will offer in the future will make it the preferred means of communication.

First, they will be powerful transmitters: the smallest of the satellites launched in the 1980s will convey several millions of bits per second,* which is sufficient to handle a tremendous phone traffic, four or five television channels, or the transfer of

the very largest computer files. With a capacity
such as this, competition from terrestrial means of
transmission will be limited to the few—certain
"Hertzian highways,"[8] future digital means of
transmission such as the "Transmic" system,[9] and
later optical fibers.[10] These systems will be able to
transmit comparable amounts of data but will be
geographically limited to a few major arteries and
be reduced in scope, as opposed to satellites capable of "flooding" countries and continents at the
same output.

Second, satellites will be universal transmitters:
in order to be profitable, they will have to be capable of transmitting all sorts of messages, including
voice, data, and images. This will be possible because the still perceptible differences between
radio satellites and telecommunications satellites
will gradually disappear as the signals begin to resemble one another. A great many projects are
taking this predictable development into account,
primarily the SBS satellite project that IBM is
planning to launch.

Third, satellites will be easily accessible transmitters: while transmission today requires gigantic
antennae (7 to 10 meters), which makes it the
prerogative of telecommunications agencies, there
is every likelihood that in the future it will become
"democratic." Infinitely smaller antennae, from
0.90 to 1.5 meters in size and thus much more
affordable, will suffice to reach the satellite.

These transmissions will also be "transparent";
they will have dispensed with the complex access
protocols* that certain land networks require today. Certain rules will be required to manage these
transmissions so that everyone will have his due in
this vast amalgam of messages. If they are limited

to technical necessities alone, however, they will
doubtless be less restrictive.[11]

Thus, the satellite will make individual telecommunications transmission possible. Faced with
these prospects, the monopoly will be reduced to
using the law to protect itself, a weak and pro-
visional weapon.

Finally, satellites will be transmitters of limitless
scope: while land, air, or cable networks are restricted by terrain and geography, satellites are
totally free of them. Most of the "shadow zones"
disappear; geographical distances are shortened.
These transmitters will inundate large regions;
borders that today are the dividing line between
national telecommunications agencies will become
purely symbolic.

Satellites will be the dominant means of communication, but they will not be omnipresent to
the extent of rendering other means of communication useless. The specialized networks in particular will still be of great importance in carrying out
certain tasks at lower cost, such as market penetration to the smallest economic entities and message switching* between small users. Capable of
connecting themselves to the satellites, they can be
used as "collective antennae" and thereby ensure
the access of these users to services that were once
off limits to them. The satellite will thus gain
further power, multiplying its influence.

**Toward "Telematic" Networks?**

Up until now, connections between computers and
data transmissions have been restricted, at least
with regard to large output, by the capacity of
telephone lines. From this standpoint, the specialized networks can overcome this restraint only
in part. On the other hand, the satellites will offer
continuous, high-powered transmission capabilities.

It will then be necessary to prepare for increasingly numerous processing transfers and data bank consultations. At the end, the network will branch out in every direction, moving toward unification.

*Acceleration of Processing Transfers*  With the exception of the still limited number of worldwide time-sharing networks,* the transfer of processing from one large computer center to another is still infrequent. The rates of speed offered by satellites will now make this possible within a single country, from one country to the next, and especially from continent to continent. A significant number of French users have stated that they are ready to transfer part of their processing operations to the United States. Presumably, they are encouraged to do so by price considerations. In fact, the time change is such that the "full hours" in Europe correspond to the "empty hours" in the United States. Furthermore, if the company offering the processing service also assumes responsibility for conveying the data, it will have a tendency to juggle the prices of both services so that the low cost of processing will compensate or overcompensate for the cost of the transmissions.

Since time changes between zones are symmetrical, there is nothing to prevent transfers from the United States to Europe as well. Given the current relative state of computer facilities and strategies, it is quite likely that transfers to the United States will remain the rule. However, the risk is that European users will become dependent on their American suppliers.

The satellites will also permit easy consultation of data banks, whether scientific, technical, or commercial.[12] A full generation ahead, with a profitable domestic market and an infinitesimal cost

margin, American data banks can offer extremely
low rates to European users. In addition, a considerable portion of the data of interest to busines·
ses throughout the world is American. The American data banks are often the most well supplied
with data on Europe.

*Interchangeability of Networks*   Shifts as decisive
as these presuppose either the interchangeability
of all of the networks or the existence of a privileged network dominating the market.

In fact, the satellite is not enough to ensure a
new "computer deal." While it guarantees facile,
high-capacity, and inexpensive transmission, it
cannot, by itself, make it possible for a certain
terminal to "speak" to a certain data bank or a
certain computer to hook up with a particular
processing center. This would require the ability
of the networks to communicate in mutually in-
telligible languages, a function that does not exist
today. Each manufacturer provides for the compatibility of his networks but sees to it that this
is not possible with the networks of his competitors. This is how "clusters of networks" are
established, which are interconnectable but cannot be connected to those of the next cluster.

Yet this heterogeneity is more theoretical than
real. It is based on the "law of the jungle," the
strongest in this case being IBM, which has the
best chance of providing these connections for
most of the networks. Its cluster will be so out of
proportion with the others that IBM will be best
able to give the phenomena of processing transfers
and data consultations a new dimension.

*"Telematics": Just Like Electricity?*   Today, any
consumer of electricity can instantly obtain the

electric power he needs without worrying about where it comes from or how much it costs. There is every reason to believe that the same will be true in the future of "telematics."

Once the initial connections are made, the network will spread by osmosis. Users will connect themselves to one another directly; files will tend to accumulate in one place when reason or profit so dictate; the transparency of the networks will gradually increase. The users will require private processing centers less and less, and the computer network will come to resemble the electrical network.

This vision is doubtless an extreme example, but it does show clearly that the linkage of satellites to networks has tremendous power potential.

In reality, some users will probably not want to give up their machines, however little they are used, in order to maintain the illusion of independence. It is also likely that the principal manufacturer will try to avoid so transparent a scheme. Less rationality, however, will not mean less power, since the uniqueness of the network will not be impaired by a few local processing operations.

Thus, within a relatively short time, the debate will focus on interconnectability. While conflicts thus far have centered on the machines, they will soon involve the domination of connection protocols. Power sharing will therefore be determined by the network manufacturers and the satellite administrators, and together they will have to define the new rules of the game.

If the telecommunications agencies launch and manage the satellites, IBM will have to establish a dialogue with them. If there are not enough of them, IBM itself will replace them, and there will be no dialogue. For third parties, this outcome would be quite effective, although less well defined.

The advent of "telematics," then, drastically affects the participants in the data-processing game, as much as it increases the stakes of the game itself.

Added to the traditional participants, that is the manufacturers, are the telecommunications agencies, and through them, the various governments. Governments have always tended to turn communications into a field of combat over sovereign prerogatives. From now on, this stretch of the ground may surreptitiously be stretched from their control if they do not provide themselves with the means to become a partner in a game where they can no longer be the master.

In the past, the stakes in the computer game were limited—they were commercial, industrial, or military. Now, with data processing dispersing into a limitless variety of small machines and disappearing behind a network with infinite branches, it is drawing society as a whole into its net.

# THE CHALLENGES

*If I had learned the technique, I would be a
technician and make complicated things. Extremely complicated things, increasingly complicated things. That would simplify existence.*
Ionesco

**Introduction**

To decide on a policy of computerization for society is to prepare for the future. To do so, the challenges of the present must be met in all haste.

This initial part of the report will attempt to inventory these challenges and to place them within the context of the crisis of French society. To do this, it is necessary to measure as clearly as possible the risks and opportunities that the new data processing poses for economic development (in chapter 3, "Telematics and New Growth"); the transformations this new data processing will bring bring about in the relations among various economic and social entities (in chapter 4, "Telematics and New Power Games"); and the expansion of the domain of national sovereignty (in chapter 5, "Telematics and National Independence").

Intuition suggests and examination reveals that the basic consequence of the new data processing is a major increase in productivity. This chapter attempts to discover the best use for the resulting surplus.

Does the computerization of society offer more risks of unemployment than it does opportunities for foreign trade? Does the increase in both foreign and domestic markets brought about by keener competition make it possible to regain or even to increase the employment that was originally sacrificed for the growth in productivity?

There is no overall, coherent, or statistical answer to these questions at present. Reason, however, along with a few projections, suggests that one thing is certain: computerization makes a new type of growth both possible and necessary.

There is no doubt that the new data processing changes the number of jobs and potentially the restrictions on the balance of trade. Depending on how it is used, it may worsen or help solve the structural problems of the crisis of French society. It will worsen them if computerization decreases employment without helping to reestablish the foreign balance; it will help solve them if by lifting the trade imbalance it gives economic policy the margin of freedom it needs to foster new growth, allowing the conflicts between external constraints, employment, and the social consensus to be resolved.

Economic models are both deficient and inherently inadequate,[1] which obliged us to proceed in the following manner:

• using existing tools to verify—with no illusions as to the accuracy of the results—the orders of magnitude of some of the findings;[2]

• working out a more satisfactory approach by outlining the area of studies vital for quantifying the medium-term effects of computerization, studies that are more sociopolitical than technological or econometric;[3]
• testing, by monograph-type surveys, the effects of computerization on productivity and employment in the most significant manufacturing and service sectors.

The findings of these investigations remain vague as to the rate of foreseeable transformation. Yet they offer some certainty about the direction, magnitude, and inescapability of changes in the next ten years that will reopen the question of the balance of trade as it was perceived when the Seventh Plan was being prepared.

**The Risk of Unemployment**

What effects massive computerization will have on employment depend on a balancing act, the outcome of a race between the reduction in manpower linked to increased productivity and the increase in markets resulting from a higher degree of competitiveness. The first effect is definite and short-term; the second is subject to conditions and will make themselves more slowly felt.

The level of employment depends to a large degree on general rationalizations effected through or in conjunction with computerization. Data processing is a second-level investment which produces profits not so much directly as by its ability to raise the value of other investments. Surveys in key sectors show that under the influence of telematics and automation the service industries will release personnel, while the large industrial enterprises will expand with a constant level of employment.

These phenomena, which have already begun to appear, will accelerate at a rate that is difficult to determine, since it will depend on the circumstances and resistance met. They introduce a disturbing new element into a process that has guaranteed the stability of the job market since the Liberation.

The remarkable gains in productivity in both agriculture and industry have made it possible for France to restore her trade balance. During the same period, the demand for jobs, which has increased owing to demographic pressure, and the entry of more women into the labor market, has not led to unemployment because it has largely been absorbed by the rapid development of the service sector with its low level of productivity. The breakdown of this adjustment mechanism, which has already begun, will continue, and at a faster rate.

No More New Jobs in the Service Sector

With telematics, the service sector will in the coming years undergo a jump in productivity comparable to the gains in productivity enjoyed by agriculture and industry in the past twenty years.

Although it is not possible to make a thorough evaluation or fix the tempo of this development, an examination of several large sectors will show its importance.[4]

1. In *banks,* the installation of new computer systems would permit employment reductions affecting up to 30 percent of the personnel over ten years, but this does not mean that workers would have to be discharged. In effect, these reductions are a measure of the numbers of additional personnel that would be required under current rates of productivity to meet the coming demand, and telematics would make additional hiring unneces-

sary. This means that the labor market will not be
tapped to the extent it has been. Indeed, in the
last year or two banks have been reducing their
hiring significantly, as compared to the previous 5
to 10 percent increase in personnel each year.

These gains in productivity can be explained by
(a) the elimination of jobs directly associated with
traditional computer processing methods, such as
"card punchers" and "adjusters" responsible for
correcting coding errors. Now decentralized data
collection coupled with self-correcting techniques
makes these jobs unnecessary. (b) The rationalization of in-house accounting procedures made possible by the new data processing, insofar as management is willing to make use of it.

In other words, the 30 percent savings in jobs is
not the automatic result of a transformation of the
computer system. Even if management wanted it,
this policy would run up against structural red
tape, individual resistance, and pressure from the
unions. There is no room for inertia, however,
since competition will force banks that may be
tempted to assume a passive role to keep up with
the more dynamic domestic banks, and even more
with their foreign counterparts.

2. In *insurance,* the phenomenon is even more
pronounced. Job savings of approximately 30 percent are now possible within ten years. Some companies, fearful of the reaction from their personnel,
have put a moratorium on the installation of telematics systems. Once again, however, it cannot be
delayed indefinitely, since the freedom to establish
insurance companies within the EEC will introduce foreign competition.

3. In *Social Security,* the movement will be
slower, since data processing is still traditional in
form, with large centers and massive, cumbersome

processing.[5] Even if no outside pressure acts to
shake the inertia characterizing its organizations,
its traditions and its regulations, then the need to
keep down costs will eventually do so. It is difficult to say how long this will take, however, when
causes are the same and effects are the same. The
likelihood of achieving job savings through telematics will be the deciding factor.

4. For the *postal services,* the foreseeable reduction in manpower is the result of another type of
competition. The new computerization will not
bring about massive gains in productivity in this
type of work, but the rapid development of telecopying and teleprinting, soon to become a reality,
and the longer-term prospect of home newspaper
publishing are all factors working in favor of a decrease in postal activity. In the initial phase, the
postal service will see a gradual reduction in domestic business and government mail, which now
accounts for 60 percent of the traffic. Private
correspondence will not be affected until a later
stage. The process depends too much on the rate
of telecopier installations, the quality of postal
services, and the service's internal labor problems
for an accurate prediction to be made. There is
little doubt, however, as to the inevitability of the
substitution of telecommunications services for
postal services and the resulting effects on employment.

5. The computerization of *office activities* will
affect the 800,000 secretaries in this huge sector
spread out over the entire economy.[6] The development of data-processing networks, telecopying,
and the incorporation of microprocessors into
typewriters are leading to a new type of secretarial
pool, one more involved in supervision than in the
performance of tasks.[7]

A relatively low investment will produce increases in productivity such that computerization will doubtless occur quite rapidly. The dispersal of secretaries and their isolation within the companies for which they work might very well lessen their ability to resist the change. The effects on employment will certainly be massive, even if the characteristics of this form of economic activity do not currently make a statistical evaluation possible.

Thus, we have five dissimilar service functions—banks, insurance, Social Security, postal and office work—with greater or lesser degrees of computerization, whose effects are sometimes direct and sometimes associated with changes in the volume of traffic, and which operate under constraints that in some cases are the result of foreign competition and in others induced by political pressures to reduce costs. Despite these differences, the conclusion is the same for all: within the next ten years, computerization will result in considerable manpower reductions in the large service organizations.

Can this conclusion be extrapolated over the entire tertiary sector? Intuition says yes, but its extent cannot yet be measured, at least not on the basis of the few projections made in the preparation of this report.

## Manpower Levels and Industrial Output

The change in computer technology will be accompanied by more rapid automation of industrial enterprises.[8] It will affect internal "tertiary" activities as well as production and will involve robotics as well as automated systems.[9]

The degree and the level of computerization of the tertiary activities of industry—administration, accounting, personnel management, and even commercial operation—differ depending on the enter-

prise. As a general rule, they are far from reaching
the sophisticated level of the systems used in banking. This backwardness is more obvious in more
recently established industries, where the rules of
management have not always been harmonized,
and it is why a broad field remains open to the influence of telematics. However, our subjects, like
their colleagues in banking and insurance, are unable to give specific figures for the manpower savings that will result from the increasing computerization of administrative operations. As a matter
of fact, it seems that in the future large industrial
enterprises as a group will tend not to hire administrative personnel.

Automation of production systems is less advanced in France than in other countries:[10] in addition to the obvious handicaps of certain branches
of industry, such as iron metallurgy and shipbuilding, traditionally dynamic sectors—including
even the automobile industry—are beginning to lag
behind as compared to foreign enterprises, particularly the Japanese.

Furthermore, under the pressure of competition,
French industry will tend to install more and more
robots[11] and production processes.* New developments in information processing place at the disposal of manufacturers small universal computers
that are particularly adapted to production management. In the same way, progress achieved in
the manufacture of terminals tough enough to be
installed in the work place will make it possible
to decentralize the execution and follow-up of
operations within the plant.

Given the increasing automation of industry,
most industrial managers state that growth in the
coming years will be accomplished without in-

creases in manpower—in fact, that manpower will decrease slightly, unless demand rises at an unusual rate. Although the restricted nature of our examination of manufacturing as compared to the service sector does not provide us with grounds for generalizing, such a hypothesis has important consequences: it means that the only industrial jobs created from now on will be in small and medium-sized businesses.

**Opportunities for Foreign Trade**

It would be suicidal to draw Malthusian conclusions from these observations concerning computerization and employment. Anything that can improve the balance of foreign trade by improving our ability to compete is vitally important for France.

External Origins of the Level of Productivity Crucial to Our Survival

The need to balance foreign trade has for many years had a prejudicial effect on growth. Any effort to achieve it under present circumstances would thwart full employment, yet increasing unemployment is threatening the social stability of the nation as a whole. This type of crisis is very new.

Until recently, growth took place within the dominant axis formed by the industrialized nations of the West. The West found an eager consumer market because of the unsatisfied needs of its own citizens.

Foreign trade accelerated growth by promoting specialization. It was the consequence of and a stimulant for development, not its condition: it often remained marginal with regard to domestic production. Transactions with the underdeveloped world were conducted so as to make it a ready market for finished products and an obliging supplier of raw materials. Favorable conditions of trade exchange increased the opportunities for growth of the "dominant nucleus," and competition existed only among nations of comparable economic and social structure. Greater capacity to compete provided a relative advantage, but differences in productivity remained narrow.

An industrial country could "choose" a tempo of productivity and growth, depending on its objectives or the constraints it faced. Except for incidental crises, easily overcome thanks to the weak resistance of underprivileged social groups, there was a harmony of long duration between growth and employment: productivity was an "endogenous" factor in a nation's control over its economic system.

Today, in the case of countries with a long history of industrialization, productivity has become an "endured constraint": in effect they are subjected simultaneously to the pressure of underindustrialized economies, overindustrialized economies, and competition for government trade.

These pincers are tightening at a moment when the part foreign trade plays in the nation's output has become essential and cannot reasonably be reduced, barring a severe recession at the same time as political coalition among the developing countries is upsetting the terms of trade in their favor. Meanwhile, new technological breakthroughs are placing some countries in a hypercompetitive position on the battlements of the future, and the low cost of labor is intensifying competition from the less developed countries in traditional markets.

As a result of this, France is being forced by the imperative of foreign trade to compete in a race over which it has no control. The search for productivity has become an exogenous factor, dominating the alternatives of domestic policy. But in order to be run effectively, this race must satisfy certain conditions.

Our Ability to Compete: "Threshold" and "Loopholes"

*Threshold effects*   If a branch of French industry, threatened by international competition (for example, iron metallurgy, shipbuilding, textiles), tries to rationalize without succeeding in reducing costs to the level of its rivals, it multiplies the constraints (massive efforts at investment, reduction of employment) without bringing about a corresponding expansion of its outlets. On the other hand, once it becomes competitive again, it will have access to new markets, allowing it to increase both production and employment.[12]

Based on computerization and rationalization, this is a policy that needs determination: it requires time and money. If its momentum is allowed to lapse too soon, before it reaches the threshold of competition, it will offer more drawbacks than advantages; it is an all-or-nothing approach. Great discernment is therefore required in choosing the loopholes to be exploited as a result of this effort.

*Choice of Loopholes*   There is no doubt that advances in productivity owing to new computer techniques are welcome regardless of where they are applied. While they have been realized mainly in the service sector, which in principle is better protected against international competition, they nevertheless stimulate the competitiveness of the economy as a whole. Some of the effects of increased productivity may carry over to sectors more exposed to international competition, facilitating their exports.[13]

However, if this productivity remains diffused, the loopholes that occupy the best positions for supporting foreign trade run the risk of being located beyond the effective "threshold." An average country cannot make itself competitive in all areas and all sectors. In an economic world in which specialization is becoming more and more necessary, an undifferentiated effort is inefficient.[14]

One must know what sectors should receive preferential treatment and which of their products should be developed, while taking into consideration the respective advantages of various other countries, enterprises that have already been initiated in one place or another, and especially the prospects offered by the market. Adroitness, which is an art that few countries have, is required in selecting the key loopholes. In Japan in the last fifteen or twenty years, and even more so since the time of the oil crisis, the "industrial-state complex" has found support in the fantastic network of data produced by the international trading companies in order to define an export strategy. Profiting from the flexibility that is the product of a high degree of social consensus, it has reoriented Japanese industry with stunning speed.[15] In Germany, these strategic choices are made by the companies themselves, which draw strength from their commercial traditions and their experience. In the United States, exports seem to be "sub-products" of a domestic market whose size and vitality provide the basis for its growth: once they are amortized, such products find a natural destination in the export trade.

French industry suffers from certain handicaps in its efforts to carry out the same strategy. Its large enterprises in many cases continue to follow broad-based policies rather than policies based on narrow

loopholes. The small and medium-sized industries
show their individuality in their organization
rather than by specializing, which would assure
them of mass production, lower costs, and greater
competitiveness.

**The Inadequacy of
Computer Technology
for Solving the French
Economic Crisis**

The French economy suffers simultaneously from
three evils: a continuous deficit in the trade
balance, a weakening of traditional domestic
demand, and a worsening of unemployment.[16]

The foreign trade stability that France experienced between 1970 and 1973 has ended with the
quadrupling of the price of gasoline. This price is
at the origin of a considerable decline in earnings,
which was not compensated for by increased exports. There is a constant risk that the resulting
deficit will be aggravated by rising imports, which
under present conditions are the outcome of any
speedup in the growth rate.

There is no doubt that the massive productivity
gains brought about by computerization will reduce our external constraints if they improve
our competitive position in a lasting way, but for
all that they will not guarantee full employment.
In order to overcompensate for the manpower
reductions that restoring competitive capacity
commonly assumes, it would be necessary to increase foreign sales to an extent that is hardly
plausible, given the world market situation.[17]

The fact is that if the effects of computerization
were limited to improving the foreign trade balance at the price of lower employment, these
effects would soon become intolerable. Social
stability would be threatened, all the more because the current crisis is dominated by two
trends of long standing. The first is temporary
weakening of demand, the short-term result of

foreign trade problems, which aggravates the basic tendency of most of the traditional objects of consumer demand to lose momentum. Progressive saturation of certain needs in the field of automotive or electric equipment and a probable lowering of investment in housing are at the source of a slowdown in the demand for basic goods. This slowdown, which has been apparent for several years, is probably going to intensify in the future.

The second trend is the growth in the active population, which will continue over another ten years in spite of the recent reversal in the birth rate, the increase in the rate of economic activity among women, the accentuation of frictional unemployment under the increasing mass of tertiary occupations, by nature volatile, and the unsuitable training provided by the educational system—all of which go along with an acceleration of the substitution of capital for labor. As a group, these phenomena are expressed in the growth since 1969 in the number of the unemployed, which was already apparent during the years of expansion (1969–1974) and has continued at a faster pace since the beginning of the crisis.

In order to provide a counterweight, the Seventh Plan has the aim of achieving marked progress in the creation of jobs, both in industry, which is expected to have 215,000 additional openings between 1976 and 1980, and more particularly in construction and public works, services and trade, and administration, where 1,335,000 additional job openings are anticipated. These are the ambitious objectives that risk being jeopardized by accelerating computerization. From now on, only a new model of growth, aimed at stimulating new kinds of demand, can offer the hope of maintaining the level of employment.

**Computerization and New Growth**

Automation and telematics will sanction such a stimulation of domestic demand as a result of the added productivity they bring and the reinforcement of competitive capacity they provide. But it is necessary to be clear about the nature and scope of this increase in demand, lest it again compromise the foreign trade balance. Indeed, there is a close connection between the intensity and the content of the new kinds of demands, the method for developing and financing them, and their effect on foreign trade. The nature of this relationship represents a social choice.

New Demands

The accumulation of traditional demand is partly related to a structure determined by inheritance and revenue. A significant transfer of purchasing power to social groups that still suffer from a low living standard would provoke some rise in overall demand for the standard items of consumption in fields like housing, cars, household appliances, and so on. However, one must neither overestimate its extent nor underestimate its effect on imports. This kind of demand cannot be expected to play a principal role in restoring levels while maintaining the balance of foreign trade.

A society less subject to external constraints would see in this situation opportunities for satisfying needs of a different nature. There is a potential demand for collective services like transportation, education, health, and amenities—culture, travel, leisure, supporting community groups, and so on. Supply will spontaneously adapt itself to demand by generating new products, transforming itself to meet new demands halfway.

The only limits to the spread of these new demands concern their potential solvency and their effect on foreign trade. Their stimulation of employment will be intense in just those branches of the economy that are least productive, and this lack of productivity will be endured because demand will focus on a sector protected from international competition.

In that respect, the shift of demand toward collective services or "new amenities," whether spontaneous or directed, promotes the creation of a maximum of employment for a minimum of imports.[18]

The mode of financing these new demands is what determines their ability to affect employment. If they are controlled by market mechanisms, if they correspond to the automatic needs of households, their solvency will come (on condition that savings will be maintained) from a lowering of traditional demand. In other words, if these demands are commercial, they will perform the useful task of transferring the exposed sectors over toward the sheltered ones without inflationary strains.

If they are deliberately guided—and consequently financed by budgetary transfers—the same result cannot be achieved unless the appropriations do not weigh too heavily on enterprises in the exposed sectors.

Thus a policy that seeks to reconcile maximizing employment with optimizing the foreign trade has both a physical limit and a political limit.

The physical limit consists of establishing a precise mix of the "exposed" sectors dedicated to maximum productivity and the "protected" sectors of the collective services and amenities,

destined to absorb a maximum of employment.
This limit is also determined by the timetable
governing their progressive substitution.

If the tilt toward one or the other of these sectors should be too strong, too weak, or even
poorly weighted beforehand, slippage would begin
immediately. Society would not tolerate excessive
unemployment, or else the trade imbalance would
stop growth again.

The political limit is set by the collective reaction
to the significance of the appropriation intended
to pay for the new demands, if the latter are not
purely commercial and are not the result of the
spontaneous development of the French economy.

Therefore, all the conditions that new growth requires cannot be met unless they rest on a broad
social consensus. They must be carefully tailored
to the specific features of each nation.

A Social Choice

The contradiction between employment and
foreign trade is felt currently by the majority of
industrial countries. It is more pronounced with
regard to those medium-sized countries that no
longer exercise domination but rather experience
its effects. Each of them seeks with more or less
success to solve this dilemma in terms of the
strong points and handicaps deriving from its
ability to compete economically and the nature
of its social climate.

The two "limit" responses are those of the countries that are moreover the most advanced in the
area of computer technology: the United States
and Japan.[19] Their choice to pursue the computerization of society is for the first the result of affluence and for the second of the struggle to
survive.

The United States predominates in the production of computer technology and its applications are the most advanced. The trade balance of this branch of industry has been strongly positive from the beginning. One can derive numerous lessons from that success, but it offers little enlightenment on how France should respond to the challenge confronting it. Indeed, the United States hardly feels constrained by the trade balance issue, both because the part foreign trade plays in the GNP is relatively small and because the monetary system enables the United States to live with a chronic deficit.

On the other hand, the Japanese approach—as it is described in studies conducted by Jacudi[20]—outlines an ambitious solution for the difficulties encountered by a medium-sized country that is densely populated, completely dependent on foreign trade, and whose main strength lies in the depth of its social consensus. The Japanese approach makes computerization central to its plan for the society of the future. Appendix 4 gives an analysis of its excesses and weaknesses, but its interest lies in the overall nature of the intervention. It seeks to answer in a perfectly coherent way the contradictions of Japanese development.

The study by Jacudi on "The Economic and Social Effects of Investment Oriented toward Computerization" tries to show on the basis of a range of criteria the beneficial effects of massive financing of information technology applied to ten specified projects.[21]

Compared to three other "scenarios,"[22] the information technology option, in which "knowledge activities" (publishing, broadcasting, forecasting, research, information technology) are predominant is supposed to triumph over every prospect, whether inflation, pollution, or congestion. In particular, it provides for notably stronger growth and a better foreign trade balance as compared to the traditional industrial option.

The defects of this project are its enormousness and its one-sidedness.[23] It certainly will not be carried out in its entirety or within its expected time limits. But it seems to be a conceptual framework able to encompass the multiple experiments being tried in Japan.

Indeed, its details are extraordinarily instructive. It involves (1) utilizing considerable public funds deducted from each household, to give authoritative support to latent collective demands (education, health, traffic, and so on); (2) as a result offering powerful and guaranteed outlets to national industries, transformed into mixed companies under private management; and (3) preparing in this way the development of products adapted to anticipated demand on the international market.

The Jacudi project is therefore intensely interventionist and innovative. It does not nationalize any sources of supply, but it does nationalize a growing portion of demand. Starting with an injection of public funds, it seeks to bend the consumption model, and in this way to simultaneously accelerate growth and exports.

It is based on a series of conditions and assumptions that have little correspondence to the situation in France: an exceptional mastery of computer technology, unique knowledge of international market developments, a very cohesive industrial structure, intense cooperation between the Ministry of Industry and the large private industrial groups, and an absence of distrust with

regard to automation. Thus this project is based
on a type of relationship between the state and
industry, a social consensus, a national determination, and an absence of individualism that does
not make it suitable for generalization. But it is
a good example of the only type of development
that can be taken seriously today, a type of
development that simultaneously responds to the
issues of growth, employment, and foreign trade.

In relation to the Japanese model, France shows
assets as well as handicaps. French individualism is,
no doubt fortunately, an obstacle to the plasticity
and variability the Jacudi project assumes. On the
other hand, it offers the hope that French households, social groups, and associations, once they
have become more aware of the paths that could
lead to new development, might be better able
than others to invent new styles of life and new
types of employment.

Thus the hope is that in France a model of consumption could be developed with less state control with regard to its objectives and methods of
financing than is planned in Japan. Its chances of
being put into effect are by no means zero. If
there is anxiety, it is caused by the time such a
transformation could require if it is to remain
spontaneous and by the limited chance it would
have of being effective if it is too authoritarian.

# 4 TELEMATICS AND NEW POWER GAMES

The social effects of telematics are undoubtedly more important than its economic effects, because they throw the traditional games of power into disorder. But they are also more difficult to encompass: one must determine what their principal motor is, whether it is computerization or society, since each of these terms is ambiguous.

In the broad sense of the word, what modifies the hierarchy or the conditions of labor is less the transformation of the machine than the evolution of the procedures and organizations drawn in its wake. Computerization is involved in a progressive rationalization of which it is both the condition and the most complete expression.

The notion of power has a double aspect. It is identified on the one hand with a series of continuously changing relationships by which the areas of competence, authority, and domination adapt to each other within a given system: in this case it is a question of "micropowers." On the other hand, the notion corresponds to the overall modes of regulation in a society—market, plan, class relations; in this case it is Power that is at stake.

Micropowers change daily and to a certain extent are modified by technical innovations. Modes of regulation are related to profound and slow-moving social currents. They may appear agitated by political "short circuits" that ratify or anticipate transformations and are inevitably transitory.

The method adopted for studying the relations between computerization and power derives from this finding. It makes a distinction between the future of a few years from now and a much more distant horizon.

Changes of very long-range nature are the subject of the third part of this report. This chapter will deal exclusively with predictable short-term consequences.

Such consequences are innumerable. An exhaustive examination of them was outside the scope of the chapter, and the proposal was therefore made to delimit certain significant sectors and analyze their response to computerization. The one ambition of this work, imperfect as it is, is to inspire by a few examples an intensified and expanded study of the subject.

The first conclusions show that information technology has today become an almost completely flexible tool. Its organization can spread without encountering a major obstacle through all the configurations of power. It will disrupt the rules and conditions governing competition among numerous economic agents; it will confirm or annul the status of positions between the center and the periphery in most organizations. But this diffused penetration will involve deep changes in essential functions (medicine, education, law, Social Security, working conditions) and by increasing transparency will raise the question of the security and privileges that issue from the shadowy zones of society.

**A Neutral Tool in Search of a System**

Traditional data processing was hierarchical, isolated, and centralized. The technical constraints were prejudicial in terms of the mode of organization which it imposed, because the presence of computers relieved the natural weightiness of the enterprises and administrations. Indeed, its procedures reinforced the center to the detriment of the periphery and the higher executive level to the detriment of the smallest units of management.

From now on, data processing can be deconcentrated, decentralized, or autonomous:[1] it is a matter of choice.

**Deconcentrated Data Processing**

For the most important users—banks, insurance companies, some businesses, certain administrative agencies—technical progress makes it possible to set up networks that can organize, around one or a few central computers, a whole architecture of intermediary machines, with outlets in many terminals installed in the most peripheral units of the organization (pay desks in a bank, collecting agencies of the Public Accountant's Office).

In such a system, the degree of freedom at the base is either nonexistent, in which case the deconcentration of data processing is a sham, or it is defined a priori and limited, in which case there is genuine deconcentrated data processing.

When the computer system is based on "nonintelligent" terminals* that cannot be programmed and therefore are only able to receive and store data, the user is not involved in the processing, which remains a matter for central or intermediary computers. For example, this is the case with electronic reservation systems: the desk attendant uses his terminal to inquire about the availability of space and to book it, as the case may be.

Such constructed networks* represent a shortening of the traditional chain, where the user transmits data to the computer service, which itself processes it and channels the answers. Thus they improve the quality of service but have no effect on the distribution of responsibilities: it is a "false" deconcentration.

If the terminal is "intelligent," which means it can be programmed and carry out certain types of processing by itself, the user will be able to perform various tasks autonomously; this is deconcentrated computerization.

Certain cases, such as collections, will at the beginning consist simply of the automation of work done up to now by hand, such as keeping accounts. Deconcentrated computerization does not by itself guarantee a broader deconcentration of responsibilities. It is the management of the organization, in this case the Public Accountant's Office, which continues to determine the distribution of areas of competence among the various levels.

In other cases, such as banks, the installation of intelligent terminals has made it possible to entrust the keeping of accounts to desk agents, which increases their responsibility.

Finally, some insurance companies expect to take advantage of the opportunities offered by computerization to entrust one agent with the entire handling of a set of client contracts. In the past, they were organized by type of disaster: a given employee specializing in automobile insurance and another in fire insurance. Here again, computerization is at the same time a stimulus and a pretext for deconcentration of responsibilities. It goes so far as to put a century-old mode of organization to trial.

In all cases, it is management that chooses the degree of freedom the units at the bottom will have. No one is entitled by his own authority to program the terminal: it is in this sense that such computerization is deconcentrated and not decentralized.

Decentralized
Computerization

The development of communication networks and the multiplication of data banks will make it possible for economic agents to have free use of a mini-computer or intelligent terminal.

For example, notaries supplied with such equipment can obtain "packages" of software, which gives them the possibility of automating bookkeeping, the succession of documents, and the clients' accounts; they can do whatever they want. The capacity of the terminal to connect up with a network will enable them also to make use of a legal data bank, a computerized compendium of jurisprudence. In the same way, they will have access to office services companies which are able to process applications their own machines are too limited to handle.

Branching offers services to independent economic agents; this is decentralized computerization.

**Autonomous Computerization**

When computers are not connected, they offer autonomous computerization in which the user is the sole master. There is no "intervention" on the part of any processing supplier or data-bank manager. In return, decentralized computerization results from the possibility of connecting the systems.

Actually, the distinction is not so sharp: one day, it will be possible to connect any apparatus. Commercial plans may lead manufacturers to avoid publicizing this capability, reserving the right to reveal the fact later on, when they will have services to offer.

The new computerization avoids the necessity of choosing between deconcentrated, centralized, or autonomous data-processing systems; if there is centralization, it is a matter of will, not of constraint. The same applies to an enterprise or a tertiary organization.

In industry, the new computerization provides for greater autonomy in the workshop; a computer regulates the tasks without referring constantly to management. However, by contrast, it may constitute a powerful means of centralization: the network makes it easier to collect basic data and follow up production operations in real time. In that case, the workers lose the limited degree of freedom they experienced under intermittent supervision; they are even more integrated into the production process.

In a tertiary organization, for example a bank, the alternatives seem to be very similar: a deconcentrated network offers the opportunity of decentralizing the entire set of client accounts, because it makes it possible to consult the files from any counter. On the other hand, a decentralized system entrusts the keeping of accounts to each agency, the central computers being used exclusively to make sure the files correspond. This choice is not theoretical: considering its atomized structure, the Agricultural Loan Society uses a decentralized form of computerization. By contrast, the three large nationalized establishments are tending toward deconcentrated networks.

The new computerization obliges an enterprise to choose its structure. It raises questions about the existing state of affairs and vested status. For that reason, it will encounter resistance.

The same phenomenon will affect economic agents, administrative services, and social categories—in fact, it will appear in any system that puts micropowers into play.

**Computerization at the Heart of Power Games**

Classic data processing remained internal to the enterprise. It did not change relations with competitors, partners, licenses, or subcontractors. In

Raising the Question
of Conditions
of Competition

contrast, telematics transforms the competitive capacity of economic agents. It improves the situation of some and evaporates the advantages of others.

The development of electronic currency, the extension of the reservation network, and the computerization of the market in perishable foods offer relevant examples.

*Electronic Currency*  Up to now, transactions between banks made less use of computerization than internal operations. From this point of view, the nontransfer of checks and the introduction of electronic currency would represent considerable progress: they would reduce the costs of processing and would make it possible to bring accounts up to date more rapidly. On the other hand, they would raise questions about the established state of affairs.

If the banks no longer exchanged checks in small amounts, they would suppress cumbersome procedures: it would be enough for them to enter the debits and the credits and inform each other accordingly. But this lightening of tasks would not be neutral in its effects: the banks that "drew" more than they "remitted" would be the beneficiaries. That is why they favor this project, while the other banks are opposed to it. Since the four largest banking establishments are divided evenly between the two categories, it is not a case of relative strength, and unless there is arbitration by the state, the disagreement cannot be settled.

Electronic currency would bring about even greater disturbances. It would imply general use of a credit card by all holders of bank accounts. A huge network operating in real time would make it possible to verify at the moment of payment that the account's credit is good. Large banks would lose the advantage of having a large number of pay desks. Indeed, financial transactions or payments could be handled in any establishment. The basis for attracting customers would be changed: the capacity to offer personalized services rather than the number of branches would be an asset. In that case, small banking establishments would benefit from their flexibility and familiarity with their customers. For this reason, large banks with many pay desks are hostile toward the idea of electronic currency.

*Extension of the Electronic Reservation System*
Up to now, reservation terminals for air transportation were installed in the offices of the airlines and their agents, and for rail transportation at railroad stations and in agencies of the SNCF (National Railways Company). Extension of the reservation system to all travel agencies does not raise any insurmountable technical problems—it requires the establishment of connecting lines. The general management of Telecommunications has already built the necessary equipment.

The extension of the network would improve service, but would deprive Air France of the relative advantage of having a great number of agents. Thus there is a conflict of interest between the national company and its agencies, which already have the equipment, and those who would like to have access to these installations.

*Computerization of Price Quotas for Perishable Commodities*   For a long time, the idea was considered of creating on the perishable commodities market a computerized information network that would distribute current quotations in order to make arbitration possible. The market at Rungis, which is of national importance, is equipped with such a system. By making the transactions transparent, the system would give an edge to consumers, who are distant from the market and badly organized. At the same time, it would whip into shape the practices of middlemen and wholesalers, who often derive real profit from the obscurity of the procedures. However, the system has never been put to work.

This obstruction is particularly sharp on the perishable commodities market, where transactions continue to be archaic.[2] It also exists for all the markets for goods and services organized in hourglass form, markets where a limited number of operators act as go-betweens for scattered producers and numerous buyers.

By providing for broader and more democratic distribution of information, telematics derails all the agents who benefit from the privileged exploitation of certain data. This produces conflicts that the state will not be able to ignore in the long run.

Power Relations in Government Administration

The effects of the new computerization on the micropowers are not restricted to economic phenomena alone. They also affect power relations outside the market, between the various administrative agencies and between the state and local communities. The network is a potential factor of domination.

All the administrative departments will not be equipped with telematic systems at the same rate of speed. The richest ones will have high-performance equipment in excess of their needs. They will be tempted to take over the transmissions of less dynamic agencies. Thus when the Public

Accounting Office manages a network that at
the beginning it will use at only 20, 30, or 40
percent of capacity, it will try to take over the
transmissions of the Ministry of Economics and
Finance, starting with the data of the general
directorate for taxes. The Gendarmerie, equipped
with a network having 4,000 access points, will be
tempted to offer cooperation to police services,
improving its position with regard to this neighbor-
ing and thus rival administration.

The unifying influence of such systems will draw
groups together in arrangements that will not
necessarily be rational. No doubt there is no desire
to dominate, but once the investment is made, the
desire to make it profitable will lead to the sub-
jugation of its clients.

The new computer technology can help to modify the relations between the state and the local
communities.[3]

The distribution of small computers will make
it possible for many communities to take over tasks
that up to now suffered from the limitations of
their financial and human resources. The development of networks is likely to facilitate new community groupings by making it possible to concentrate means and disperse utilization.

Telematics also plays a role with regard to the
relations between the state and the localities. It
can encourage either atomization or organized
groupings, thus either maintaining state control or
limiting it.

Public authorities, as we shall see, must provide
themselves with the means to remodel the structure
of administration and not let themselves be carried
away by the swift current of centralization.

**The Issue of Social Status**

The new computerization will in the future have an aggregate effect on whole groups, for example, on the medical profession and on the teaching profession. It will also affect professional qualifications among the working class. These changes are very likely to bear on the way collective interests protect themselves.

*Computerization and the Medical Profession*[4]

Telematics can change the characteristics of medical intervention, the conditions of medical practice, and some of its traditional values.

By making medical care less expensive, computerization risks the possibility of "medicalizing" a large portion of the population, so that the slightest indisposition will become a pretext for a large number of medical examinations. Every social ill will look toward medicine when the traditional structure of the profession is put into question.

Indeed, computerization will break up specialties by restoring to the general practitioner functions he was not able to perform in the past. For example, he will be able to interpret an electrocardiogram, partly replacing the cardiologist. The greater accessibility of medical treatment will not be limited to transferring skills from the specialist to the general practitioner. It also blurs the borderline between the role of the physician and that of the medical aide. The responsibilities of the medical aide will increase; in some cases, he may even do entirely without assistance. Thus, in anesthesia, automated installations will enable him to bring a patient back to consciousness by himself. Even if as a result of this physicians gain time to devote themselves to nobler tasks, they will feel that they have been deprived of a portion of their professional function.

Computerization may modify the position of the medical practitioner with regard to his environment. When eventually a network is set up connecting the pay offices of medical insurance agencies with doctors' offices, it will transform the practice of the medical profession. Economic considerations will be more pressing and will reduce the physician to the more modest status of a provider of services.

Computerization also raises the issue of maintaining privacy in medicine and calls for special precautions in that respect.

*Computerization and the Teaching Profession*  The overall impact of computerization on education has not been analyzed within the framework of the present report. However, it may be of some use to draw a hypothesis on the subject.

The development of computerization on a mass scale may transform pedagogy and thereby the status of teaching personnel. The computer and the network themselves will not be the teaching tools that some people expect them to become. The educational formation of a student is not limited to the communication of technical information. No robot, regardless of how well programmed it may be, will be able to conduct the unique dialogue that occurs between teacher and taught.

The computer nevertheless aids us with artificial intelligence, which may modify our relation to knowledge. With its help, the student will be able to deal with complex problems that are closer to reality. Statistical analyses will not be limited anymore to simplified calculations, and the scale of simulations will be infinitely greater. Little by little a different relation will develop, consisting of dialogues and successive repetitions, each of which will sketch out an original thought process. If this change is pushed to its extreme consequences, it will transform teaching. What will notions like school curricula, preestablished courses, and gaps between disciplines mean when the rhythm and even the kind of teaching will vary from one student to another?

This development, for which few minds are prepared, would have effects on teachers similar to those experienced in their turn by physicians. Specializations will fade away and levels of teaching will become diversified, modifying the rigid statutory requirements on which diplomas and grades are based. Education will see its function distilled to one of coordinations, while more routine pedagogical tasks will be carried out by assistants. Looking at the matter from this point of view, a whole sociological world will undergo transformation. Given the state of mind of the teaching profession, it is not surprising that this development is not self-evident; it would not in any case be rapid.

*Computerization and Professional Qualifications*
The new computerization affects working conditions; therefore it also includes manual workers. It changes the behavior the workers adopt to defend their interests and poses new problems for trade union action.

Working conditions change by following a dual movement.[5] Automation gets rid of some menial occupations and lightens tasks. In addition, it leads to disqualification of many types of work performed up to now by highly skilled manpower, for example printers; installation of automatic machines devalues the skills of their trade. The printers themselves are replaced by ordinary supervisors, probably signaling the end of the labor aristocracy. These effects take place over a long period of time. To detect them would require a penetrating analysis that only peers could carry out.[6]

Standardization of the tasks will undoubtedly be accompanied by new forms of hardship. More the result of boredom and a certain amount of monotony, they will be psychological rather than physical; the work will be experienced differently.

Such developments will take place at the moment when computerization will be affecting employment. The conjunction of these phenomena will in time change the central themes of trade union action—pay levels, work hours, job titles, and employment. More than that, it will involve the difficult game of unifying claims and the defense of categorical interests, a game that is about to be renewed.

**A Strategy of Counterforces**

The effects of computerization on the functioning of society will be decisive and may be formidable. It is thus important that public power, once it has been made aware of the risks involved, encourage the vitality of counterforces. Above all, it should conduct this policy in its own domain, the civil service.

The risks involved in computerization with regard to civil liberties are self-evident, and they are also often underestimated. What is less recognized are the conveniences computerization can provide. The public authorities must avoid responding to fears concerning civil liberties by blocking efficiency. The point is that they must be reconciled.

**Civil Liberties and Efficiency**

For the general public, computerization amounts to keeping files, an activity prejudicial to private life and liberty. That is one of the aspects most capable of arousing passion and one of the best explored among the consequences of computerization. The computer and the card file have assumed a symbolical value that crystallizes allergic reactions to modern life. These fears have been explored thanks to the notable studies conducted by the Commission on Computerization and Civil Liberties, the parliamentary debates they made possible, and the proposed legislation that was the result.[7]

However, during the Occupation, the Gestapo did its job rather efficiently, without having interconnected electronic card files at its disposal. And Sweden, which has the richest and best-referenced files of any country, runs little risk of becoming a police state. This means that, in this matter, the quality of the social fabric, pluralism among the forces at work, and the play of counterforces prevail over the "freedom-killing" traps of technology. Legislative provisions resulting from the studies of the Tricot Commission attempt to institutionalize some of these counterforces. The best future is one where society accepts the advantages of computerization, its efficiency, and its ability to simplify life, while providing an imperturbably democratic climate to oppose its indiscretions.

Civil Liberties, Openness, and Vulnerability

A more open society, better knowledge of collective and individual states of affairs, is not always bad. Profits, privilege, and fraud find nourishment in obscurity. A democratic society would suffer from seeing information on people's private lives, their religious or political opinion, and their morality entered into card files or even utilized. But would it function better or less well if the revenues of this or that corporation were known with more precision because of better data-processing techniques? It is paradoxical to say that in France some people think that it is freedom to be able to conceal what one earns, while in the United States it is frustrating not to be able to know how much one's neighbor earns. The goal should be to support the liberty of all by openness, rather than to preserve the privileges of a few by allowing concealment.

If society is sufficiently democratic to allow the emergence of counterforces, if it is sufficiently mobile to organize the fight against the "new delinquency" that may come into being as a result of computer techniques,[8] the risk is not one of openness.

The risk is elsewhere, in the fragility of society as a whole. Modern management tends to multiply nerve centers, and a short circuit in one of them can paralyze huge organizations. A too centralized, too structured, and too hierarchical use of data processing would tend to multiply this vulnerability to "grains of sand," whether they are accidental or deliberate.

The role of public authorities is to support the forces counteracting these centralizing tendencies, particularly within their own administration. As of today, one must centralize only what has to be centralized, fragment anything that can be fragmented, and deal with essentials right away, reserving only exceptional matters for action at a higher level.

Thus the government cannot limit itself to promoting equally all the modes of organizing data-processing techniques. The pressure in the direction of structured, centralizing networks is so strong that it is necessary to counteract it. Some people claim then that the government engages in a discriminatory policy by favoring the promotion of decentralized, small-scale computerization. Yet it is the only way of maintaining some degree of autonomy and responsibility for the weakest actors on the social stage. However, since in a medium-sized country the reorganization of power assumes a margin of freedom with regard to foreign governments and groups, who might oppose such a move, it calls for a minimum of sovereignty in several strategic areas.

Telematics renews and increases the stakes of independence. No doubt the latter resides in economic health and social consensus. Some prosperous countries are satisfied with this. Others, more concerned about their stability, more nostalgic for former power, or more desirous of preserving their influence and their freedom, try to safeguard their autonomy in certain key sectors. It is from this perspective that the turning points of data processing—the development of networks and the creation of data banks—call for new actions.

**A New Industrial
Imperative**

The Policies of
Yesteryear

Since the appearance of the first computers, data processing has become a strategic sector in most countries; conscious of the specific character of its raw material—information—governments quickly became interested in this industry. In fact, since 1945 few areas except the atom have received such close government scrutiny; this vigilance was an expression of the wish to limit American domination, stronger here than in any other area. Governments devoted major means to this end, each following a strategy in conformity with its own temperament.[1]

Japan set out to gather the technological knowledge necessary for the manufacture of computers. It then closed itself off to all outside meddling, setting up a Draconian protectionism. Guaranteeing outlets for its data-processing industry, it based its growth and exporting capacity on mass production.

Germany, for its part, accepted American predominance right from the start. Little by little, once the basic technology had been acquired, it set about "Germanizing" the products: this is a policy it has followed in other domains, such as nuclear energy. It was thus able to forge a solid industry, positioned on export battlements.

Great Britain has followed a diversified policy: the decision to support a national manufacturer made up one element of an overall plan of action in which the development of applications, the training of users, and links with telecommunications held important positions.

France has carried out a Colbertist policy. The desire to build the computers necessary for the *force de frappe* made its willed character even clearer. This effort was concentrated on a single undertaking, set in the administrative domain, spurred on by a desire for technological independence, and managed according to mechanisms that closely intermingled industrial objectives and government constraints.

Strategies as diverse as these had to produce unequal results. The accelerated computerization experienced by all these countries left a more or less large share to foreign products. In 1975, American companies supplied 45 percent of the computer pool in Japan, 60.5 percent in Great Britain, 75 percent in Germany, 83.5 percent in France (after the C11 Honeywell Bull merger, 75 percent). These overall data mask dissimilar phenomena: more or less developed technical potential, unequal exporting capacities, and differentiated repercussions on other data-processing sectors. The ironies of history have thus made the French services industry the second in the world, while at the start this was not a prime objective.

These contrasting situations show that the battle to reduce the position of American industry is already over, a battle aimed first and foremost at IBM because of its dominance of computer manufacturing. Today the challenge is different—IBM is going beyond data processing, and the stakes, the field of battle, and the nature of the competition have changed.

**Transformation of the IBM Challenge**

In order to face up to IBM, it is necessary to understand the reasons for its dynamism, to measure the weight of its success, and to try to anticipate its future direction.

This company has played the multinational game more intelligently than any other. Supported by the American market, the world's foremost, it has known how to invade the markets of other countries.[2] It decentralizes its industrial and commercial activity but retains control over its essential strategies in research, investment, and marketing.

It dominates the sector expected to undergo the greatest development in the coming decades—data will continue to expand in tomorrow's society, and data processing and later telematics will accompany it. IBM is entrenched, if not alone at least with such reserves of power that it cannot be seriously threatened. Unlike the petroleum groups, it is menaced neither by suppliers who could catch up with it from behind, nor by cartel partners whose solidarity does not exclude rivalry, nor by the uncertainties and hindrances experienced by all the conglomerates.

Its place (60 to 70 percent) in the world computer market reveals its technical and commercial capacities and explains its financial strength, which supports a policy that holds all the trump cards for penetrating the data-processing market from above and below. No firm, and no government either, has so mastered the chain extending from component to satellite.

Up to now, the source of IBM's success has been its commercial dynamism. It has submitted rigorously to the play of the market, guiding it along, yet giving in to it. For IBM, as for all data-processing manufacturers, the future will demand a different sort of activity. IBM has followed the twists and turns of the new data processing as much as it has given rise to it.

The world's foremost user of components, IBM has also sought to be the foremost manufacturer. It has succeeded in this with impressive speed and efficiency. Henceforth the company will attach exceptional importance to telecommunications. This was shown by its determination to obtain from the U.S. government the right to launch a satellite.[3] But communications will hereafter be too overlapping and satellites too important for IBM to be content to engage in teleprocessing. Once it has committed itself to transmitting voices, images, and data, it will be led to compete with the telecommunications organizations in their traditional sphere of activity.

Any government or private company that tried to respond to this strategy by concentrating exclusively on computer manufacture would be opposing yesterday's IBM, not today's, and still less tomorrow's.

The industrial response—we shall return to this later—concerns all aspects of the data-processing profession: components, manufacture of mini- and paracomputer equipment, large-scale data processing, and service companies. But the sovereignty stakes have shifted to control over networks, which condition both communications control and the direction of the computer market.

Paradoxically, IBM's success and the field of its new development provide governments with the opportunity to take their place as the company's

intermediaries in an area where they are not so
defenseless. Manufacturing and selling machines,
IBM had customers and a few rivals. As a con-
troller of networks, the company would take on
a dimension extending beyond the strictly industrial sphere: it would participate, whether it
wanted to or not, in the government of the planet.
In effect, it has everything it needs to become one
of the great world regulatory systems.[4]

Some organizations have been or are bearers
of an eschatology that ceaselessly tries to rearrange
its operative machinery: for example, the Catholic
Church or the Communist International. Today
each of them is seeing or experiencing the difficulties this constant hubbub presents. Starting from
the reverse situation, IBM has a calling to become
in its turn one of the great actors on the world
stage. At this very moment it has the equipment.
It may be trying to hasten the commercial prospects for such a development; it is undoubtedly
not measuring the political constraints. The extent
of its success will sooner or later oblige IBM to
take a new view of its environment; this will offer
national governments the opportunity to open up
a renewed dialogue with the company.

Most of them are poorly prepared for this contest. They need to become aware of its novel character and strengthen their bargaining position with
a solid mastery of their communications media.
The difficulty lies even more in the fact that no
country can play that role alone.

States were formed to establish within their
boundaries an acceptable balance between the
great economic and social rivalries. But the inter-
nationalization of the stakes means that today
no economic Gallicanism is sufficient to keep
Rome out of Armonk.[5] Independence would be

vain and as easy to outflank as a useless Maginot
Line if it were not supported by an international
alliance having the same objectives. Such a policy
is not easy; neither is it out of reach, as we
shall see. It would naturally be in the interest of
all the players in the data-processing game, whether
public or private. Each nation would thus retain
the freedom to pursue its own societal projects.

On the other hand, the lack of governmental
action created a void, which was quickly filled by
the dynamism of IBM. If IBM were now to be
"sucked in" by societal problems having political
overtones which do not form part of the logic of
its industrial and commercial development, it
would be distracted from its vocation. In extending its domain over sectors under public control,
it risks stirring up resistance and undermining its
commercial effectiveness.

IBM should try to obtain negotiations that will
clearly define the boundaries between governmental prerogatives and the market. It is to be
hoped that the spokesmen involved will be powerful enough that IBM will neither designate them
nor take their place. It will thus be up to the state,
and insofar as we are concerned up to France, to
establish this front of spokesmen for the public
interest.

**Network Sovereignty**     The development of network systems renews the
old problem of relations between the state and the
communications media. This is not a simple reflex
of authority, wanting to use telematics to shore up
its prerogatives. The multiplicity of the economic
agents it puts into contact, its ability to aid information exchanges, and its role as an instrument of
power explain its importance. Without control,
the state will not be able to overcome the effects

of network domination or preserve sufficient freedom for each of the participants. Computerization would then be subject to influence of communications media administrators, who, for legitimate reasons of profitability, would basically seek to lock in their customers.

If several manufacturers of comparable importance shared this task, it is possible, despite the risk of a cartel, that they would neutralize each other. But the omnipotence of IBM throws the game off balance—IBM would determine the mode, the rate, and the attributes of computerization.

Controlling the network system is thus an essential objective. This requires that its framework be designed to serve the public. But it is also necessary for the state to define access standards; otherwise the manufacturers will, utilizing the available routes but subjecting them to their own protocols.

In order to maintain the advantage this policy will gain them, the public authorities must immediately start preparing for the satellite phase. From this double perspective, they will find potential allies in the "telecommunications international."

The Power of Standardization[6]

The objective is to ensure open exchanges by allowing users to converse among themselves independently of their equipment. Otherwise, they could not use the hardware or services of another manufacturer. In fact, guaranteeing connections, despite the heterogeneity of both hardware and software, requires, first of all, defining common rules for the handling of messages, a form of standardization that involves the telecommunications function. But it is also necessary to unify the form in which they are broadcast and find some sort of common language and syntax. This implies specifications that encroach on the manufacturers' domain.

The level of standardization will thus shift the boundary between the manufacturers and the telecommunications organizations: it will be a bitter struggle, since it will develop out of a reciprocal play for influence. But the objective of public control indicates the strategy to follow: increase the pressure in favor of standardization.

Such a line of action, however, assumes two preconditions. The first is standardization of protocols. A complete absence of standards would be better than purely national rules. These would isolate French economic agents, depriving them of foreign connections and services and weakening their ability to compete. Further, French manufacturers would be unable to export their equipment. The second precondition is the capacity to bring all the participants to accept these constraints. Standardization constitutes a cage. If IBM did not enter, then shutting up any one of its more flexible or more dependent competitors would amount to a penalty.

No doubt the choice of such a policy can slow down the rate of technical progress: creating a durable set of unifying rules in the face of a rapid and almost uncontrolled process of development involves a delicate balance.

However, given the fact of the dynamic vitality of the manufacturers and the probable reticence of some telecommunications organizations, an ambitious policy of standardization would not excessively thwart innovation. Beyond this, it is in any case important to prepare for the fundamental satellite stage.

Satellites

Intended as the pivot of communications, the essential link in the development of network systems, and aimed at facilitating the increase in overlapping transmissions, satellites are at the heart of telematics. Eliminated from the satellite race, the European nations would lose an element of sovereignty with regard to NASA, which handles the launching, and with regard to the firms that specialize in managing them, especially IBM. By contrast, if they were capable of launching them, building them, and managing them, the same nations would be in a position of power. This supposes a framework of action beyond the reach of any one country.

Building satellites is the prerequisite. European industry today can produce weak satellites; from now on, it needs to prepare itself for the next generation, which will alter modes of transmission.

These satellites must not constitute simple "mirrors" reflecting data from one point to another, without rules for handling and transmitting messages. Network system manufacturers would otherwise no longer be constrained to respect the principles of free access. Hence it is up to the various nations to implement protocols, playing a role analogous to that of the X 25 for ground networks.[7] This effort will run up against the traditional obstacles. The excess costs that these standards will impose on open lines, the risk of thwarting technical progress, and the difficulties of implementation are so many counterarguments.

However, without satellites, national governments would no longer be participants in the development of telematics. Yet without protocols, the satellites they could construct would amount to vain alibis.

Designing and building platforms is not enough: the satellites must still be launched. By depending on American rockets, the European countries would benefit from aid all the less warranted in proportion to their satellites' capacity to reinforce a far from negligible element of sovereignty. Without yielding to an obsession with conspiracies, it is necessary to watch out for possible convergences of interest and prevent dependence from developing in a crucial area—the launchers—while an effort is under way to limit it elsewhere, in the telematics networks. The Ariane Program seems to be going in the right direction, but it is not within the scope of this report to judge whether it may be able to place powerful satellites in orbit during the years 1985–1990.

In any case, such a policy can only be conceived within an international framework. It is too costly for a single country, while the definition of protocols at the satellite level requires broad accord, as does any standardization measure. Here, too, as with ground networks, a vigorous policy is needed if France is to find allies.

Potential Allies

The multiplication of international transmissions has required permanent cooperation from the telecommunications organizations. Investments made in concert, definition of rules and procedures, and the rise of financial interdependence give rise to a common approach. Certain specialized instances (CEPT at the European level, CCITT on a worldwide scale) form the traditional framework within which this telecommunications "international" finds expression.[8]

It has undoubtedly experienced tensions and cleavages. The German telecommunications administration is apparently restive about drawing up a European satellite policy: it would thereby lose the transit fees guaranteed it by its position in the heart of Europe. Likewise, adoption of packet-switching techniques* for data transmission has not been unanimous: Great Britian, Holland, and Spain have rallied to it or are in the process of doing so, while the Nordic countries remain partisans of circuit switching.* These conflicts will remain sharp so long as the problems they reflect are part of the telecommunications world.

In the face of potential rivals, the international is being reformed. This was demonstrated by adoption of the X 25 protocol for standardization of data transmission: the accord was concluded despite pressure from the computer manufacturers. The minimal solidarity is one that would create a partnership among the European nations. It would carry more weight in proportion as it received support from AT&T. Today this seems possible because of the growing competition IBM will exert over this "empire."

In short, European national sovereignty may be reinforced by joining with an American telecommunications firm whose situation makes it close, in terms of its structure and interests, to the European administrations. Of course, the risk remains that AT&T might reach an accord with IBM concerning the American and world markets, or even an agreement to share power in the world market alone, despite the lively competition they might give one another in the United States. Under such a hypothesis, the European administrations would be weakened. But this is not very likely. The interests of these behemoths are divergent; their

structures and their past histories make them alien
to each other.

**Independence through**
**Control of Information:**
**Data Banks**

The appearance of network systems has given rise
to the development of data banks, which are
multiplying, especially in Canada and the United
States. Meanwhile France is beginning to fall far
behind in this field.[9] The public authorities
need to undertake vigorous action; failure to do so
can create a dependence that may have heavy
consequences.

A Risk of Alienation

Data banks change the conditions of statistics
collection and retention: they infinitely expand
the capacitiy to store data, whether it is a question
of conserving raw data or bibliographic references.
They modify access requirements and make
remote examinations possible, so long as they can
plug into a network.

This phenomenon strikes squarely at the whole
of economic, technical, scientific, and academic
activity. The same is true for the small firm,
which henceforth will be able to go to a specialized bank to find such and such a manufacturing
process, and for the forecasting arm of a large
company, which will have available all the data
concerning the outlook for economy. All of these
data existed before the installation of data banks,
but most of the time they were scattered, unman-
ageable, and difficult to use. It is ease of access
that creates the need. Two users, one of whom
makes intelligent use of data banks while the other
is content with sparse traditional information,
find their positions in the economic game modified as a result. It is the same for academic work,
or the search for commercial loopholes by a large
firm.

Data banks are often international, and the
development of transmissions allows access to
them without excessive tariff penalties from any
point on the globe. Hence the temptation in some
countries to utilize American data banks without
setting up their own.

Indifference to this phenomenon is based on the
belief that this dependence will be no stronger and
no more disturbing than for any other type of
supply. But the risk has a different character.
Information is inseparable from its organization
and its mode of storage. In the long run, it is not
only a question of the advantage that may be
conferred by familiarity with such and such a set
of data. Knowledge will end up by being shaped,
as it always has been, by the available stock of
information. Leaving to others—i.e., to American
data banks—the responsibility for organizing this
"collective memory" while being content to
plumb it is to accept a form of cultural alienation.
Installing data banks is an imperative of national
sovereignty.

A Data-Bank Plan

Data banks are not all alike. Some may remain the
property of closed groups and professions whose
members are not very numerous, while others
must be accessible to everyone, under penalty of
affecting the balance of power. The former are
intended for the few, while the latter support, for
example, national forecasting and planning. The
first develop solely by the initiative of future
users, while the second require vigorous involvement on the part of public authorities. The
creation, diffusion, and regulation of access to
these data banks conceals a problem of a political
nature. This report cannot deal with all the legal

and ethical questions raised by this rapid development. Only their general orientation warrants being underscored: it is not clear that all the major departments of the government—the universities, INSEE, the technical ministries—have perceived the strategic importance of data banks. Witness, for example, the little use that the major French economic institutions make of the international banks, although they would seem to be the base on which to build a national equivalent. Under these conditions, it is the government's responsibility to take the initiative and to give legal and financial support to the entities competent to carry out this task. Such action would gain in breadth and effectiveness if the public authorities developed a data-bank plan, verifying the institutions to be created, avoiding useless cross-checking, and determining those responsible for implementing them. This is the policy followed in particular by the German Federal Republic.[10]

# II POINTS OF SUPPORT

*Only innovation hastens a State.*
Montaigne

**Introduction**

It is necessary to give the government an instrument of power, but also to incite its wielders to adapt to their new market. This is the subject of chapter 6, "Telecommunications."

The government must also aid the other players in the data-processing game without taking over their positions; this is the subject of chapter 7.

Computerization of the administration may freeze it. Conversely, data processing may help it to do less, but better; this is the subject of chapter 8.

# 6

Telecommunications are the obligatory point of passage for computers whenever they communicate with one another. Implantation and management of systems will determine most of the economic, industrial, and social effects of the new data processing. Their capillarity may facilitate territorial reorganization. Their tariffs will arbitrate the respective interests of the large and small firms; they will facilitate or control the access of households to new services and thus the benefits they receive. The politics of network systems will decide whether telematics remains the activity of some few powerful fiefs or is distributed democratically.

But telecommunications are not solely a neutral vehicle for messages; they can serve as the support for transmissions protocols. Depending on how ambitious the standardization policy is, they can "surround" data processing, making its associated equipment seem commonplace, freeing captive customers, restoring consumer freedom, and equalizing competition among manufacturers. Initiator of a concerted strategy for a "telecommunications international," the French pole must become the instrument of a less lopsided dialogue with IBM on the problems of sovereignty.

This policy presupposes a long-term plan on the part of the government and strong bargaining capacities, but also dynamic executive organizations, flexible and sensitive to the market. These prerequisites today remain unsatisfied. The government spreads its forces too thin and leaves them without coordination. The way Transpac has succeeded shows, by way of example, the nature of the immediate stakes and the reforms they imply. The latter may go so far as separation of the postal

service and telecommunications and the creation
of a Ministry of Communications coordinating
the long-term action of all the participants.

**Absence of a Unified
Strategy**

The current situation allows poorly arbitrated
rivalries to establish themselves with no clear distinction between regulatory power and administrative functions.

Multiple Participants in
Contradictory Positions

Unlike most other countries where transmissions
depend on a single authority,[1] telecommunications
has a general monopoly, which by waiver excludes
the radio and television system managed by Télé-
Diffusion de France (TDF). Satellites involve in
addition the National Space Studies Center (Centre
National d'Etudes Spatiales—CNES), in charge of
launching and building them, and the Ministry of
Industry, which, since it is concerned with their
export, is interested in their mode of use and
hence in their general nature. Supported by departments inspired by their technological enthusiasm
to engage in lobbying, agents of the interests of
their technical personnel, these organizations form
subtle alliances for competing or contradictory
objectives.

Mighty in its power—25 billion francs in turnover, 130,000 salaried employees—assured of its
immediate future thanks to an investment plan of
100 billion francs within five years, the General
Telecommunications Directorate (DGT) sees in
Télé-Diffusion de France a historical accident that
it must circumscribe and in the end circumvent.
Having on the contrary only one billion in turnover and 3,500 agents, but benefiting from the
financial advantages conferred by holding a monopoly over a growth market and a cost-based tariff

system, TDF aims at multiplying its services, to
differentiate itself from the DGT and thus become
indispensable. It seeks alliances that will prevent
it from having to confront its cumbersome rival
head to head. Hence it sees in the CNES a potential ally for a satellite policy removed from the interests of the DGT which would also be a means
for renewing its legitimacy. As for the CNES,
while it deals with TDF and DGT in only a portion
of its activities, the weight of each leads it to side-
step a dialogue with the stronger DGT and set up a
balancing act by relying on TDF.

It is in terms of data transmission—today over
ground networks, tomorrow by satellites—that the
competition will be most lively between TDF and
the DGT, whence the bitterness of the contest for
control over space platforms. The options to be
decided will have long-term effects, and they depend on highly technical considerations.[2] In the
absence of competent argument, these difficult
questions will require arbitration by the prime minister's office, without the intervention of all the
critical analyses apt to be used to facilitate decisions whose logic would dictate they be introduced as a last resort, not in the first instance.

Scattered
Administration and
Confusion between
Regulatory Powers
and Executive
Function

The place of the telecommunications organizations
in the administrative structure fluctuates with the
rhythm of governmental reorganization. While
the DGT remains riveted to Postal Service and
Telecommunications, TDF was attached to the
Government Press Office, and after its disappearance, directly to the office of the prime minister.
For its part, the CNES depends on the Ministry of
Industry.

This administrative dispersion makes a common
policy difficult, even impossible. Divergences are

kept quiet and remain hidden, allowing each organization to pursue its own policy. Arbitration by the prime minister's office, when it takes place, become all the harder as TDF is directly under its tutelage.

These various organizations, however, enjoy a very concentrated power: they simultaneously provide for the regulation of public service and its execution, playing the role of both actor and guardian. This confusion stands out by its singularity. Countries such as Great Britain, the United States, Canada, and Japan have long understood the distinction between the power to guide and regulate and the executive function.[3] This situation prevents the telecommunications pole from becoming the instrument of a policy. It harms both the power of public authority to provide long-term guidance and the organizations' industrial and commercial adaptability.

Imposing a coherent direction on this sector as a whole requires in particular dissociating the regulatory from executive tasks and distinguishing the transport function from that of service.[4] Transpac illustrates the necessity for these reforms.[5]

**Example of an Immediate Task: Making Transpac a Success**

Development of a data-transmission system and the search for a high degree of standardization are, as we have seen, the backbone of a communications policy. This is the ambitious task that the public authorities have assigned to the DGT with the construction of Transpac. It is to be operational in 1978 and gradually to be extended over the entire territory: its objective is a broader diffusion of data processing, easy and inexpensive access, and an increase in the services provided to users. It may promote faster standardization. Its success is essential.

Yet considering the nature of the current market for transmissions and its likely future extent, it is obvious that Transpac's success will be neither easy nor sufficient. It presupposes a profound transformation of the DGT's traditional business practices and a whole new game with the service companies. These needs are not very compatible with current structures. Furthermore, Transpac is only one stage, fleeting and limited, in a long-term standardization strategy.

A Marketing Operation to Accompany Service Activities

*A Marketing Operation* Recourse of major users to Transpac will not be spontaneous: many of them bring up the low capacity of the lines, the sophistication of the access protocols or secrecy problems to avoid making a choice. The argument is ambiguous.

The major organizations, already reasoning within the hypothesis of future transmissions by satellite, prefer to keep their specialized lines during the interim period and thus avoid the constraints of linking up with the public system. Some, however, wish to make partial use of it so as to benefit from its branches in the most distant areas. This option would leave the least profitable part of the traffic to Transpac (transmissions with the most isolated bank branches, for example; links with outlying factory workshops). In practice, this would make major users the equivalent of small users.

In the face of these major clients—essential because they condition Transpac's profitability—the DGT must take more of a commercial than a technical approach. Such is not the case today. Thus the Public Accounting Office launched studies preliminary to the installation of an autonomous network totally independent of Transpac. In the perspective of an active data transmission strategy, it would have been a risk to see a public service carry out a sniping action. The government would have lost all its arguments for convincing others to rally to Transpac.[6]

The problem is even more acute with regard to small and medium-sized users. If the DGT does not succeed in attracting them, data processing's penetration will be dangerously slowed down. The DGT's tactics are delicate: they cannot be as personalized as with the large firms, nor can they use as an argument the special benefits the DGT could offer. It is in no position to seek out a clientele whose only motive in joining up is to have access to certain services (data banks, possibilities for shared time, additional memory capacity). It is not up to it to install such systems: its size and ponderousness make it hardly capable of the flexibility required by an uncertain and mobile market. On the contrary, it must back up the development of these services. On this point, the DGT, in order to succeed, needs to form alliances with other promoters.

*A Service Strategy*   The development of telematics will be accompanied by a multiplication of technical possibilities: electronic mail, televised message services, access to data banks, home newspapers, video conferences, and so on.[7] During the next few years, the market will make allowance for limited-use gadgets and major services. However, the public authorities are not out of the picture: profitability analyses, market studies, and recourse to user panels will be able to help them make choices. Thus studies done at the request of the DGT show the coming importance of electronic mail and the rapid switching of institutional mail, the internal correspondence of administrations and businesses, from the traditional postal service to the electronic postal service.

These perspectives are important, for they affect the industry's potential markets, allowing mass production of inexpensive devices, highly standardized and therefore suitable for export.

Flexibility on the part of the DGT, persistent market surveys, ample commercial services that are both mobile and decentralized, the ability to depend on the service companies as natural intermediaries for small users—such are the stakes for the swift and satisfactory spread of Transpac. These are the challenges for which a traditional administration is ill prepared. To respond is not within the competence of technicians alone, even highly skilled ones, nor of administrators, even if they are outstanding. In other words, Transpac's success, taken as an example of transformations in the communications network, depends on internal institutional change. But even this would not be enough.

The insertion of telematics into government administration and the promotion of services for which the DGT would be but one support call for coordination in order to harmonize policy. Its goal would be to choose the services, weigh the costs and drawbacks, and entrust one organization or the other, TDF or the DGT, with control over the process and responsibility for project development.

This impetus is even more necessary, as Transpac's profitability period is counted in years, and as its standardizing effects will be in vain if they are not conceived as a transitory stage.

An Inadequate and
Transitory Stage of
Standardization Policy

By benefiting from the capillary of the telephone network, practicing equality in public service, and improving the balance between major entities and small and medium-sized users, Transpac can be the tool for as democratic as possible a diffusion of data processing. But this implies a high level of standardization.

This is why, so as to facilitate the linking up of the small users and above all to preserve some freedom for them in the choice of services, Transpac is supported by polyvalent protocols which will allow wide access to its networks. Thus it will be possible for two parties using data-processing systems produced by different manufacturers to communicate with each other.[8]

First of all, it is necessary in the international cases of CEPT and CCITT to promote the adoption of the "virtual equipment" protocol.[9] The battle may be rough. It would enlarge the attributes of CCITT at the expense of the international data-processing organization, the ISO, which is a vehicle for the major manufacturers. It would presuppose the definition of complex rules. It would run up against the joint opposition of some governments and manufacturers. Even if these obstacles weaken the chances for an international accord on a virtual equipment protocol, an active policy within the "telecommunications international" remains no less essential; its fallout will inevitably take the direction of increased standardization and stricter protocols.

If this cannot be achieved directly, the DGT may succeed in establishing a de facto virtual equipment protocol. For this, it will be necessary to develop software to make systems compatible, in connection with competent service companies. Still embryonic, this policy would gain a new lease on life if it had the support of a power pole. Telecommunications can lead such an action: it benefits from the required technical competence, substantial financial means and a central position conferred today by its monopoly.

The eventual success of this policy leaves the future open. It does not guarantee. If this action on the ground system does not prepare the stage for the time when protocols of the same nature could be imposed on the management of transmissions by satellite, France, as we have seen, would have won a battle but lost the war.

**Prosecution of a Communications Policy**

If the public authorities are to gain control over communications policy, the organization charged with carrying it out must coordinate their activity and pursue it energetically.

**Making the Activity of Telecommunications Organizations More Dynamic**

No doubt telematics represents but one dimension of telecommunications. Measured by the number of subscribers, the level of investment, and by turnover, it seems marginal alongside the massive effort invested in telephone equipment. However, the importance of its customers, the weight of its economic effects, and the stake in sovereignty it represents all make it a significant enough domain to serve as a legitimate basis for certain questions concerning the management of telecommunications.

It is true that telematics is particularly demanding. Managed within the framework of a monopoly, it functions in one that resembles competition. If a candidate for the telephone does not obtain satisfaction, he cannot turn to another supplier; in contrast, if the available connections do not satisfy him, a potential Transpac subscriber may find a temporary solution and wait for satellite linkups. The success of the DGT in telephone equipment will be a result of its capacity to carry out a program based on productivity. Its success in telematics will depend on the subtle leadership it exerts within a network of alliances and associations. Such a policy is unusual for a monopoly sure of its legitimacy and preeminence and would require several adjustments.

1. The DGT must adopt a business approach. The policy of a monopoly often consists of distributing a product without being concerned beforehand over the needs of the customer. Transpac on the contrary is requesting a market survey of the clientele, the offer of services likely to justify the linkup, and finally facilities for joining major users in a study of "tailor-made" branching.

2. The DGT hence must expand its recruiting to high-level business executives. To integrate them firmly into its manpower pool, it will have to adjust its salary indices. Beyond the hiring conditions, time and effort will doubtless prove necessary before the new recruits are accepted by engineers naturally inclined to give a higher status to technical work.

3. If the DGT does not take commercial market criteria into account and requires Transpac to sell products developed without reference to them, failure is likely. Thus a cycle involving "market targets" and technical constraints is necessary. If it intends to engage in a dialogue of equals with IBM, the DGT must develop an approach that is not completely divorced from its interlocutor.

4. To apply it will require institutional modification—better adaptation of personnel and the possibility of redistributing tasks without coming up against unwieldy statutes. This unwieldiness has less to do with the existence of a statute than with its maladaptation. The agents operate in effect under the general rules of government service, so that problems of parity are constantly being posed: between telecommunications agents and clerks with-

in the state secretariat, between officials of this ministry and those of other departments. These difficulties are even more acute as the inclusion of technical jobs in salary indices based essentially on administrative work is not easy. The specific nature of telecommunications must be taken into consideration.

5. Given the "working masses" of the DGT (130,000 agents today), centralization is incompatible with executive flexibility. Decentralization of its current administration, a portion of its investment, and recruitment is unavoidable. Unless this happens, it can hardly hope to satisfy its customers: marketing plans are not battle orders, and an "army" cannot carry them out according to its usual procedures.

These imperatives have been analyzed with regard to Transpac. But is it desirable to seek flexibility for Transpac alone, or should this metamorphosis be operated on telecommunications as a whole?

The recent decision to create a joint company for Transpac shows the beginning of awareness and may constitute a step in the right direction. But it is hardly realistic to imagine a small, commercially oriented service back to back with an immense, bureaucratic administration. The agents of the one are pledged to one day becoming the agents of the other; financial procedures become intertwined; and support for Transpac's commercial activity will mostly be furnished by the DGT. Furthermore, Transpac does not constitute an isolated investment: it is the telephone that guarantees its extension over the territory as a whole, just as the growing overlap between types of transmissions is erasing the sharp distinctions between the data transport network and other systems. Finally, the

problems of telematics have effects that go beyond
Transpac. They suppose, as we have seen, coordination between the DGT and TDF and a satellite
policy. Under these circumstances there is no
solution for the Transpac system alone; it is the
management of telecommunications itself that is
at issue.

This brings up an old debate: the sharing of a
single ministry by the postal service, which is
labor-intensive, and telecommunications, a highly
capitalistic enterprise. Technological development
accentuates the dilemma. Telecommunications will,
in time, deprive the postal service of its most profitable activity: transport of institutional mail
along the most heavily used routes. The two services will henceforth be not only different but
competing. One will experience problems of stag-
nation or even regression, while the other will
benefit from strong growth. The postal service involves the preservation of a monopoly that has
hardly been breached, the management of a large
force of manual labor with low productivity, and
the need to prepare for difficult times. Telecommunications involve mastery of ever more sophisticated tools, the task of facing up to powerful
private competitors, most of all IBM, and the obli-
gation to act aggressively in the marketplace without letup. The postal service will be obliged to
weigh the argument of manpower costs, while
advances in productivity registered by telecommunications would allow it to carry out a more
generous salary policy to which parity constraints
are the only obstacle.

Separation of the two administrations is thus a
virtual certainty. If the public authorities do not
continuously guide it, one day it will become a
situation fraught with tensions and difficulties.

The ultimate objective is the creation of a national telecommunications company, but its realization presupposes a progressive evolution. Pressure from a political leader can transform an administration but a revolution cannot be imposed overnight. Many stages are possible: creation of two appended budgets, one for postal and financial services and the other for telecommunications; establishment of personnel statutes more in harmony with technical imperatives; and decentralization of responsibility for the most important program areas.

**Toward a Ministry of Communications?**

The scope of the policy to be carried out, its international ramifications, and the importance of the organizations under trusteeship require a high-level authority. What should its jurisdiction and structure be?

*Content of the Trusteeship*  Two misunderstandings should be avoided. First, the trusteeship for radio and television programs must be outside the authority in charge of communications policy. Joining together under a single authority the broadcasting networks, the "container," the transmissions, and the "content," could give rise to legitimate concern.

Second, coordination does not mean fusion. Once the sharing of tasks has been clearly effected, it would be proper to grant to each organization a right guaranteeing its own expansion. As soon as the border wars were finished, the trusteeship should utilize TDF to experiment with peak techniques and new markets, protecting it from the pressures of its big rival.

It is a question of delimiting the business of each: the authority charged with communications policy should be responsible for developing policy options—choosing the means and defining the tasks. For this it needs budgetary prerogatives. To it naturally falls the exercise of the monopoly, the enunciation of an industry policy (standardization of hardware and software), and the overall distribution of investment. It is also up to it to define, without considering the market, the principle applications, to make the essential tariff decisions, and to ensure a political dialogue with the users.

In return, this trusteeship should forego any meddling in the management of the executive organizations; their activity could be staffed by program contracts or company plans leaving them a great deal of autonomy.

*The Instruments of a Long-Term View*   The complexity of the decisions requires that the trusteeship have a fairly ample economic service so as not to depend exclusively on studies carried out by the executors. This strategic unit should clarify for the decision makers the options available to them.

The trusteeship could be supported by a research institute studying the long-term effects of communications. Its economic, sociological, and cultural consequences should be analyzed; today this is not being done anywhere. Some centers deal with it here and there.[10] None of them, however, feels responsible for these questions as a whole nor enjoys formal administrative support; above all, none is placed within the sphere of a decision-making authority.

*Structure of the Trusteeship*   A Ministry of Communications must not take the form of the current department of the Postal Service and Telecommunications, rebaptized and reinforced by TDF trusteeship and a partial trusteeship over the CNES. Too monopolized by the postal service and overextended by the effort to equip the telephone network, it would have neither the aptitude nor the means to carry out a communications policy. A few schemes can be submitted for consideration:

*a.* The least innovative solution would involve maintaining, alongside the Ministry of Communications, a state secretary for postal service and telecommunications who would preserve all the department's prerogatives. He would thus take up directly from the ministry only IDF and for a part of its activities, CNES. But under this hypothesis relations with the DGT would go through a state secretary, powerful and monopolistic: the debate between an idea-producing ministry and a state secretariat charged with managing would inevitably be ambiguous and unbalanced, a source of slowdowns and disorder.

*b.* A more vigorous alternative presupposes the nomination to the Ministry of Communications of a state secretary in charge of postal and financial services. In this way, the DGT would depend direcly on the ministry. This formula would allow development of a coordinated communications policy, as it would involve a single trusteeship. Transforming the DGT into a national company is part of this scheme.

*c.* If the public authorities preferred the institution of a general communications delegation attached to the prime minister, they would encounter several difficulties. The delegation might find itself assigned the trusteeship of TDF and partially of the CNES. In contrast, its relations with the DGT would be equivocal.

If the DGT were the object of a double attachment, to the state secretary for postal service and telecommunications on the one hand and the general delegate for communications on the other, the latter could in theory exercise his prerogative of coordination. In fact his hierarchical superiority to the director general of telecommunications would be uncertain: since both would be named to the Council of Ministers, they would be at equivalent administrative levels. The delegate, while endowed with theoretical power, would not have very ample outside services at his disposal; his subordinate, the director general of telecommunications, would continue as he does today to direct an industrial empire. Conflicts would be certain.

If the DGT remained under the exclusive control of the state secretary for postal service and telecommunications, the general delegate could only exercise his function of coordination by asserting the primacy of his arbitration in the name of the prime minister. This situation is not inconceivable, as the behavior of DATAR proves. However, it presupposes unfailing support from the prime minister so as to prevent the state secretary for postal service and telecommunications from demanding unceasing arbitration from the head of government.

The installation of a delegate risks giving a too technocratic tone to the authority responsible for communications policy. The size of the stakes and the importance of its international partners, whether public or private, require a political authority. Creation of a Ministry of Communications is therefore in the final analysis preferable to a simple delegation.

# 7 THE GOVERNMENT AND OTHER PARTICIPANTS IN INFORMATION PROCESSING

By strengthening telecommunications, the government extends its field of action. By making computerization of the state administration part of a larger prospect, it could, as we shall see, set the pattern for a future in which the sphere of government action and the sphere belonging to society are better distinguished. Thus it could establish within its own domain the boundary between direct intervention, more circumscribed but more active, and allowing the participants free play.

In the face of consulting companies, makers of mini-, para-, and large-scale computer equipment, component manufacturers, and research institutes —that is, all information-processing activities outside the administration—such a distincition is even more necessary: the government must leave them the greatest possible margin of freedom. Its role will be more or less decided according to the situation: without substituting for them, it will aid them in performing their work, sometimes defining the terms for this, and will act promptly when the case calls for it.

Today, the public authorities face three problems.

1. Unlike the large-computer industry, which was built up deliberately, certain branches of information processing developed by themselves. The service companies are potentially the second largest branch worldwide. In mini- and paracomputer equipment, several small manufacturers have sprung up, without however reducing our strong dependence on foreign countries. But these activities are still very scattered and include enterprises at different levels of development. Their insertion into an overall computer policy is not simple.

2. This computer strategy presupposes undertaking action in the fields of research and the

manufacture of components. Certainly these two sectors have different natures—one is disinterested and detached from market phenomena, the other is highly competitive—but they pose similar questions: how to improve our know-how in areas where knowledge evolves rapidly and draw the consequences for industry. This shared question evokes different approaches.

3. The last nongovernmental actor is the large-scale French computer industry. It is a problem in itself, but also the fruit of traditional, complex relations with the government.

**Scattered, Dynamic Enterprises: The Service Companies and the Mini- and Paracomputer Industry**

Service Companies[1]

*Solid Know-how* The service companies (SSCI) were largely born out of the pricing system imposed by the manufacturers in the earliest ages of data processing. Billing only for the hardware, and later for certain software, the manufacturers provided the installation, which they did not charge for, and the demand for which never stopped growing. They welcomed the development of companies taking charge of that function. The SSCI subsequently removed themselves from the manufacturers' orbit. Technical assistance to the users is progressively giving way to the development of software applications, the role of consultant to that of foreman. At the same time, "office services" activities are reinforced, offering the advantages of subcontracting and availability during disruptions. Diversification of the tasks of the SSCI has accompanied their rise. Specialized sometimes in terms of their technical potential, sometimes in terms of the number of their customer groups, and sometimes in terms of the nature of their financial constituents, today they offer a complete range of services. These are distributed in two broad categories, machine services and intellectual services. The first

group assembles all the processing activities:
"office services," scientific calculations, and consultation of data banks. The second goes from
technical assistance and dispatching of qualified
personnel to the conception and installation of the
most complex systems.

The French SSCI often hold the leadership of
the profession in Europe. The reasons for such industrial success, all the more remarkable as it is
rare, are multiple: the arithmetic plan has favored
the development of software, which the CII, concentrating on computer-manufacturing problems,
subcontracted; the establishment of branches for
data-processing services by large banks and large
firms offered a captive market; and a certain distrust of the manufacturers was in the end able to
facilitate recourse to less tutelary third parties.
These favorable factors take nothing away from
the credit due to the marketing know-how of the
SSCI and their qualities as an industry.

*A Major Trump*   In addition to the privileged role
they may play in standardization, the SSCI provide
an alternative to users and are a means to reach
new clients among small and intermediate users.[2]

The manufacturers are shifting their approach
through the installation networks. For them it
offers the assurrance of furnishing their hardware
and software, maintaining them, and in particular
providing future extensions, because of incompati-
bility with other systems.

This is why state activity cannot be limited to
installing a public data transmission system and
broadening access to it. It is necessary to free the
users from the manufacturers' monopoly over the
design of large systems architectures. This would

allow the grouping of hardware and software from the most diverse sources.

From this viewpoint, the SSCI represent a major trump: some already possess the capacity to develop the most sophisticated networks. Some seek to slip into the interstices of the manufacturers by developing compatible software. All of them should take advantage of standardization so as to intervene in networks originally conceived by others. Thus the user will have freedom of choice, with several possibilities available, some developed by the manufacturers, others by the services companies; the market will decide.

Development of small computers responds to the needs of the many atomized users. Even if they become accustomed to data processing more quickly than did the large organizations, these new users will nevertheless start by requiring simple, traditional tasks of their machines (payroll, accounting, inventory, access to professional data banks). Under these conditions, software applications are not of major complexity. They might be very ordinary: nothing should more closely resemble the payroll of some small enterprise than its competitor's payroll. Facility in technical development and an interest in the emergence of standard products give an advantage to the SSCI. They can in fact respond to the needs of the market; they benefit from the mobility and flexibility conferred on them by their reduced size. They are also capable of satisfying the concerns of clients wishing to personalize some software or other.

*Supporting the Service Companies* There is no need at all for the government to substitute itself for dynamic SSCI. On the other hand it must contribute to their efficiency by offering them markets, helping them to export if they need to, and giving them the means to become involved in communications policy.

The SSCI benefit little from government orders— 17 percent of their turnover as against more than 50 percent for their American counterparts. This situation is injurious. The state administration in effect represents its main support. Its size leads it to order major and costly systems; its technical requirements amount to pledges of quality and thus function as references in the foreign market; and finally the permanence of its needs is equivalent to a guaranteed turnover.

Concerned about establishing their authority over substantial services and then meeting union pressure to increase public jobs, those responsible in the state administration hire agents to carry out tasks that they could subcontract. In their eyes, administrative work seems free of charge, and any external allotment therefore seems abnormally expensive.

Only a governmental policy based on time and effort can modify these practices. The external assignment of certain kinds of work would support the SSCI; it would also have the merit of disengaging the government from activities for which it is not well equipped.

There are as many problems in terms of exports as there are for allotments. For processing, extending French networks abroad is necessary so as to counterbalance the influence of foreign companies on national soil.

The SSCI might find government support for software and the large systems. Exporting SOFIA not only involves selling a data-processing product, but even more, furnishing a set of customs procedures. Likewise, a large network like that of Direction Générale des Impôts (tax department) or the CNRS reflects a revenue system or the management of a scientific organization. Exporting is equivalent to promoting an administrative technique. Under these conditions, the government should help companies on the foreign market. It could play on its capacity for diplomacy, and especially on the favorable context that cooperation can create.

The communications policy offers openings to the SSCI: linkups to Transpac, the creation of compatibility protocols, the development of new services, and the installation of data banks. The mobility and creativity of these companies will lead them to multiply their involvement. In effect their interests and the government's converge, the commercial expansion of the former reinforcing the exercise of the latter's prerogatives.

**Mini- and Paracomputer Equipment**

Mini- and paracomputer equipment will be support markets in the future.[3] But who will profit from them?

France is very dependent on foreign suppliers, especially American. It satisfies only 20 percent of its needs in office computers and 40 percent in terminals and universal minicomputers. This branch of industry nevertheless comprises some dynamic firms which have acquired a fairly solid position through exports.

Growth in demand will be such in the future that without a strong national industry the foreign deficit will increase. But in such a lively sector any protectionism would penalize the national economy. Furthermore, the scattered state of the constituent firms makes public action difficult.

The government must thus carry out two policies, one of stimulation, the other precautionary.

1. The procedures for assisting mini- and paracomputer equipment have just been usefully coordinated in the form of growth contracts. Putting into play public resources infinitely lower than those allocated to the large-computer industry, they nevertheless permit backing up the development of the contracting firms and helping them over certain thresholds. It is not certain that these funds measure up to existing needs; the capital of these companies is scanty and their capacity for self-financing limited.

2. There is enough market support for the principal French manufacturer, CII-HB, to receive its rightful priority as an axis of development. The evidence shows it would be unhealthy to forbid them to manufacture French mini- and paracomputer hardware, which is the normal complement of large computer networks. However, the weight of the company's financial and industrial capacities and previous commitments made in its behalf will make it a crushing competitor for the small paracomputer firms.[4]

The government's role is thus to keep the growth of the one from being achieved at the expense of the others. It is imperatively necessary for all the participating French firms to prosper and reconquer part of a market until now largely controlled by their foreign competitors.

**The Acquisition of Knowledge and Know-How: Computer Research and Components**

Up to now, research has been entirely oriented toward creation of a French computer industry, contributing to the collective effort to develop domestic hardware and software. The activities of the CII and the IRIA complemented each other. Today,

Computer Research          research is at a crossroads: the merger of CII and
Honeywell Bull has allowed creation of another
market-oriented firm whose research work will be
guided primarily by commercial objectives.

Will there consequently be room beyond industrial research for basic research? What type of development should support it? What strategy can the
government adopt? These questions call for more
expert answers than those in the present report.
But basic research evidently remains indispensable.
Telematics lends added weight to problems of
standardization, compatibility, and portability
that require basic study. A policy turned toward
the future must not be based on industrial research
alone. Basic research may follow either one of two
models, in data processing as in other scientific
domains.

1. In some countries, it consists of a thick fabric,
connecting research centers, universities, and private firms in a web of contracts and information
sharing involving an intense exchange of workers. This is, to define it briefly, the "American
model." It requires great flexibility, great permeability between institutions, and insignificant
social cleavages.

2. Research may also result from a powerful,
structured activity administered from a pole of
power. This might be called the "CEA model."

Each of the two firms of organization has its advantage and fits in more or less well in a given
country, or within a single country in a given sector, as determined by outlook and tradition.

In the data-processing realm, French research
centered on the CII and the IRIA has depended
rather on the second approach, which is more
Colbertist. Today, the shift in industrial policy is

an opportunity to reopen the debate. It would surely be desirable for research to expand in a more decentralized fashion, but at present this seems unlikely. Nothing is impelling data processing to enjoy an institutional mobility that has not come to characterize other scientific activities. Hence it is necessary to resign ourselves in the name of efficiency to a centralized research model.

What remains is to find the pivot. In the telematic universe, a single organization, the CNET (National Center for Telecommunications Research) seems likely to play such a role. It is at the core of the coming changes; it has solid teams; and finally it benefits from the financial bonanza of the "telecommunications plan."

Of course, the country has an interest in creating a living and dynamic interstitial fabric. From this viewpoint, the IRIA can play a guiding role.[5] Its mobility and its flexibility should allow it to issue contracts, multiply exchanges, and create a research climate and community suited to the future, especially in the area of data-processing utilization.

Components

Components paradoxically raise the same questions as data-processing research: Is it necessary for them to play a strategic role? If yes, how to go about it? Is France in a position to carry out such a policy? Regarding the strategic nature of components, authorized opinions diverge.

To some, it is a question of sovereignty. In the future, a cleavage will appear between the countries with mastery over component technology and those without it, analogous to the ever more pronounced gap between the "nuclear" nations and the "non-nuclear" nations. Integrated circuits will have major applications: they will penetrate into the sectors of high-consumption goods and perhaps revolutionize its products. Aside from this general use, they have a function specific to data-processing, since the difference between a component and a small computer is increasingly tenuous. Without a components industry, will data-processing manufacturers perceive technological changes in time? Manufacturers of integrated circuits will become producers of minicomputers. Abandoning this sector is equivalent to counteracting efforts to help mini- and paracomputer equipment.

To others, components have no strategic significance: the market is vast enough to permit everyone to have some of it without financial penalty or risk of penury.

Our technical expertise in this area is weak. It seems to us, however, that renouncing setting up a components industry carries an immense risk. What is needed is to get one started. To do this, several methods come to the fore. One of them depends extensively on state planning and protection and is based on governmental guidance of one or two firms profiting over a long period of time from public credits and reserved markets. Another method depends on a large number of small, dynamic firms. In countries where they exist, some have experienced a dazzling success; many have failed.

There is no basis for choosing between these two policies. For research, a centralized and structured form of action seems required. Components, however, seem to call for a more flexible involvement, more oriented by the logic of the market; the brevity of product generations and the absence of a size imperative militate for this approach.

However, weakness in technological know-how and the absence of manufacturers ready to take the risks in such a venture make state action difficult. It is not up to the government to encourage a network of small firms, to import the know-how, to carry out complex patent and tax policies; in this game, it risks setting up "arsenals." It needs industrial relays. Only the large groups involved in the field of electronics can lead such a project and, for example, buy one or two American component firms. Against this they have the inconvenience of their size and a para-administrative approach. There is a risk, if size prevails, of falling back into subsidized arsenals.

Even if action in this direction were decided on, a double contradiction remains between the need for state support and the need for a mobile and dynamic sector, between the ineluctable involvement of the great industrial groups and their initial handicaps.

**Large-Scale Data Processing**

Large-scale data processing has for ten years formed part of the government's traditional realm of intervention. Today it is expanding within the framework of the CII–Honeywell Bull accord, which seeks to place the French effort in a competitive realm and modify relations between the government and the national manufacturer. The public authorities contribute major funds to CII-HB to allow it to establish itself on the market and subsequently survive there on its own.

This raises several questions. Some are linked to the firm and its capacities in the face of competition, others to the relations between CII-HB and the players in the data-processing game, and the rest to the possibility of associating the national manufacturer with a wider strategy.

The problems proper to the firm have to do first of all with the complexity of the data-processing industry. A merger is difficult: it presupposes technical prowess so as to ensure the compatibility of the products. This is even more complicated as the accord provides for technical exchanges between CII-HB and its American shareholder. Finally, there is the need to amalgamate the teams without traumas or second thoughts. Achieving these objectives is made harder by the market's structure, the alliances formed there, and any setbacks that may occur.

The operation has hardly been launched, and the perspective to make an overall judgment is lacking. Furthermore, these questions bring into play the discrete strategies of the firm and the government. It is under this heading that they should be treated.

The weight carried by the national manufacturer gives the nature of its relations particular importance. In effect it could interfere with the data-processing strategy of the public authorities, especially in terms of telecommunications. It risks being in competition with the minicomputer firms and service companies.

Like any manufacturer, CII-HB is concerned with the goverment's standardization policy. If it is not careful, the firm may be its victim. Standards must in effect weigh equally on all, and especially on IBM. If the latter succeeds in escaping them, it would be unhealthy to subject one of its competitors to them because it is more docile. On the other hand, CII-HB and the DGT can support one another on the technical plane, providing each other with data and conducting research together, taking advantage of their common nationality.

With the minicomputer firms, the national manufacturer has different relations. As a powerful competitor for the business of more modest participants, it must be very prudent in avoiding the perverse effects of an unbalanced struggle.

The SSCI poses comparable problems. CII-HB is as of today the foremost French service company; manufacturing standard software, it competes with some SSCI. The public authorities must be attentive to this situation. A national manufacturer as powerful supplier of services is a trump; a manufacturer, national or not, that monopolizes some types of services would in contrast be a handicap.

In the long run, the public authorities could utilize the national manufacturer to reinforce their telematics strategy. But there is still another precondition: waiting to see the first effects of this policy.

If the government succeeds with other governments in imposing standardization on the manufacturers as a whole, including IBM, CII-HB itself will have a share in profiting on the commercial plane from the situation thus created. In effect, the user will be freed, which opens up the market to the smallest—CII-HB—even more than to the largest—IBM. At the extreme, the French manufacturer would win a guaranteed compatibility of his machines with those of IBM.

It is the capacity or incapacity of the government to carry out the data-processing game that is the determining factor; reinserting the national manufacturer into the public strategy will then take care of itself.

# 8 THE COMPUTERIZATION OF GOVERNMENT ADMINISTRATION

In addition to its sovereign prerogatives, the government is the largest service enterprise in the country. In this double role, the relations between the administration and data processing are vital.[1]

As its biggest customer, the administration affects all those engaged in the data-processing profession (manufacturers of machines and of networks, service companies, and so on).

As a user, the administration is subject to the full impact of the effects of telematics. It may passively accept these hand-to-mouth; it may also take the occasion to redirect its evolution.

The choice between these two attitudes is vital for society as a whole. Actually, data processing is more "structuring" in the administration than in any other organization, and the administration remains a dominant model by its influence and its role as an example.

The choice, however, is not easy. If the public authorities allow data processing to penetrate in a disorderly way, they preempt the future. On the other hand, no global scenario can be imposed from a single center without suffocating society or paralyzing the government. Therefore, it is necessary to conciliate a maximum of freedom and a minimum of coordination, to facilitate change rather than to impose it.

**Noninterference: Arresting Future Development**

Although left to the spontaneous initiative of each department and moderated by preferential prejudices deriving from industrial politics, the spread of data processing through the administration has been extremely rapid.

But it has taken place in a very uneven way, strengthening barriers; this is all the more worrying because it immobilizes the structures that it penetrates for a long time.

Uneven Development    The purchase of computers has never been regarded
by the administration as an investment. Two con-
sequences follow from this.

First, the resources devoted to it are not those
required for massive equipment outlays over short
periods of time but ordinary departmental resources.

Second, in the absence of a correct accounting
for the cost of such outlays, resorting to outside
assistance, for example, to a service company,
appears to be prohibitive.

Thus, in the case of major projects, the administrative departments that have the means to do so,
hire numerous teams, whose employment is no
longer justified when it is a question of operating
the system that was installed. But this plethora of
data-processing staff of very good quality in some
places has as its counterpart a scarcity of them
elsewhere. Actually, only the most powerful
departments can attract and keep these technicians.

For example, the taxation administration was
able to recruit and train within its own organization the personnel for its data-processing centers.[2]
On the other hand, the limited interest generally
shown by magistrates in management tasks and
limited budgetary resources explain the mediocre
automation in the Ministry of Justice; this is not
unrelated to the difficulties faced by that department in confronting the increase in its tasks.

Between these two extremes, there is a whole
range of contrasting situations, from the most
advanced data processing to its total absence, from
effective data processing to pure waste, and from
the most sophisticated data processing to the most
unsophisticated. The more traditional and richer
departments, such as the Ministry of Finance, the

armed forces, and the police, are ahead of the
departments serving the public: education, health,
justice, and local communities. Wherever the
machine has been unable to make up for the in-
sufficiency of human resources, the quality of
service has been lowered.

Compartmentalized
Development

In the majority of cases, each department acquires
data-processing capabilities without worrying
about the possible difficulties that its plan may
cause elsewhere, and especially without measuring
the "synergistic" effects that better coordination
with other departments might have produced.

Thus, hospitals have developed systems for billing medical expenditures and hospital-stay expenditures without collaborating with Social Security.
Within Social Security itself, its compartmentalization into three branches, each of which develops
its own data processing, has led to manual retrieval
of data produced by the computers of the other
branches.[3]

As a result of the present departmental separation, the Direction Générale des Impôts and the
Direction de l'Aménagement Foncier et de
L'Urbanisme (land development and urban affairs)
each establish a land data bank, the former for
tax purposes, the latter for development purposes. The legal definitions and the types of
information differ; nevertheless, there are broad
common areas, but nobody worries about them. In
addition to the waste, the establishment of these
two data banks prolongs administrative isolation.
Strengthened by this investment, both administrations are prepared to resist attempts at a rapprochement. Data processing makes it more difficult to
set up a single land administration in the future,

when it might be desirable to do so. The opposite process would have been more fruitful. If a single authority had been able to examine the future of land administration, it would have used its influence to try to set up a single bank, in order to plant the seeds of a future rapprochement.

A Decades-Long
Rigidity

A period of over a decade separates the first studies concerning a large system and its operational installation. For example, SOFIA, an automated procedure for clearing goods through customs,[4] has been operating at Roissy and at Orly since 1976, that is, nine years after its design. Nine years were also necessary to extend data processing to the administrative and medical management of patients at all the intensive-care hospitals managed by the Paris welfare department. Such examples could be multiplied; there is no large system presently in operation that was not designed before the end of the sixties. In fact, without an agreement to increase the resources devoted by the government to investment in data processing, the implementation of a project will freeze a department for several decades.

To continue in this manner will not guarantee effectiveness, since redundancy and duplication, a surplus of resources here, unfulfilled requirements there, and budgetary requirements everywhere do not assure the best public service. Compartmentalization multiplies the procedures and steps for the user. This does not preserve freedom: authoritarian departments will always find the resources and the credit to procure their equipment, and to reestablish such interconnection capabilities as they may deem necessary.

This mechanism is cumulative. Following the current path, the "strong" (a powerful office, a central administration) will become stronger, and the "weak" (an office without resources, an external agency) will become weaker. The present scenario, if it is prolonged, will lead to a future that no political deliberation has planned and that no authority, should it ever wish to do so, could easily modify. The administration will have been surreptitiously shaped by this course for the next twenty years, through hundreds of conflicting good intentions.

This situation is made more serious by the fact that the government is not simply one organization among others. In France, it is a pole of attraction, a contagious example. It conditions the shaping of the institutions placed under public authority (universities, hospitals, Social Security and HLM agencies, and so on), most nationwide industries, and the local communities, as well as many other industrial or tertiary organizations whose conduct remains under state control. Through the use it makes or does not make of data processing to loosen the traditional hierarchical pattern, the government will design the framework within which most of the great bureaucracies will be managed in the future.

**Illusions and Dangers of Imposing a Model**

Data processing offers the means to implement the most diverse schemes, the "Tout-Etat" (complete centralization of state control) as well as that of extreme decentralization. Thus guiding the acquisition of data processing means selecting a model of society. It would be illusory, and even dangerous, to believe that such a choice, and, a fortiori, the option of decentralization, can be imposed by an all-powerful center, building a global scenario piece by piece.

The "Tout-Etat"
Scenario

Data processing evidently may make the "Tout-Etat" scenario plausible: that is its risk and for some its temptation.

The scenario would be based on a multiplication of the flow of information essential to the control of a vast and complex system. Its highly hierarchical organization would be designed to fulfill the requirements of the "center." It would then be possible to establish the vast data-processing system that some people are now envisioning. It would be based on the allocation of a unique identifier to the elementary units represented by men, companies, and land. The use of such an identifier would be mandatory in all files. Interconnection, obtained by means of permanent links, would make possible an almost instantaneous retrieval of the elementary information. The only irrational features would relate to unsettled departmental conflicts.

This arrangement is advocated by some Soviet economists. They believe that the introduction of sophisticated data-processing networks would make it possible to alleviate the rigidity, the incoherence, and the waste of centralized planning. This is a myth. The will of the state is multiple, and most often incoherent, because it is expressed by the infinite number of basic administrative units. Their coordination requires innumerable decisions, which nullify one another, get entangled, or are settled by the ultimate holder of power, who arbitrarily crushes the others or becomes glutted and chokes.

Nobody in France would dare advocate such a scenario. But innumerable pressures lead naturally to it. There is an explicit unanimity about criticizing its consequences, but an implicit agreement to push for its implementation; the technical stratum's dream of rationality and the majority's desire for equality combine to expand the power of the state and its satellites.

**The "Decentralizing" Scenario**

Rejecting this future means causing and anticipating a double evolution: that of a government that would organize its own demise and that of a civil society taking care of needs fulfilled until now by the public authorities. It also means discarding an illusion.

Decentralization evokes deep-seated reactions. The power attained by the state apparatus—what some call social control—is the result of a movement started several centuries ago which has accelerated to a breathtaking pace in the last few decades. Without doubt the flourishing of experiments, the emergence of the ecological movement, and the vitality of communal life demonstrate a new affirmation on the part of civil society. These initiatives combine in a Brownian motion an anti-state attitude based on principle, the defense of certain private interests, and a bucolic nostalgia. They refuse to take responsibility for the stability of society as a whole. Often, they express a desire to enjoy both the delights of life in the country and the advantages of postindustrial civilization.

It is therefore illusory to expect decentralization to be produced spontaneously by society but even more so to imagine that the public authorities can organize their own demise from a single, central will. The government cannot impose change; it has to create the conditions under which others will be able to produce it. By the institutional unrest to which it gives rise, data processing, properly used, may provide leverage for this evolution.

**Facilitating Change**

No administrative, central, supervisory, hierarchical organization can assume the prerogatives of the departments without causing resistance and stoppages. It is not possible to concentrate in the hands of a single individual the design and the execution of data-processing systems for the entire administration without multiplying rejections or errors.

On the other hand, no major enterprise—and what enterprise is larger than the administration?—neglects establishing a unit to analyze and forecast the evolution of its functions, under penalty of sclerosis. The government, however, does not do so. Certainly, each agency thinks about its own future and therefore about its own data processing. But current tasks are pressing. If it released the spirit of innovation, it could only do so within its own world. It would need to possess a peculiar virtue to question itself.

Certainly, the budget office partially plays a synthesizing role among the departments, but its own constraints naturally lead it to emphasize short-term considerations. With respect to the RCB missions,[5] they deal with problems that are too limited to be used as the nucleus of a more ambitious policy.

Therefore, it is necessary to create a body and procedures for inducing the public authorities to question themselves about the future of their departments. This function, which cannot be hierarchical, must consist of analyzing the present and envisaging, in close cooperation with the agencies concerned, coherent and alternative projects, thus enabling the government to make real choices in due time. The agency entrusted with this "maieutic" of the future must be a delegation for administrative reform attached to the office of the prime minister.

Composed of a few high-level personnel for its planning activities,[6] the delegation should not exert any coercion. Its task would be to analyze, warn, alert, propose, and persuade.

In addition to the problems of reorganization, which the delegation would consider on its own authority, it would participate in all work preceding any institutional change. In case of disagreement with the project in progress, it would have the right to appeal to the prime minister for a decision. On the other hand, to support the projects that it finds desirable, it would use the resources of a modest fund to cover part of the expenses of reorganization, which are usually charged to the overhead of each department.

The most important decisions would be taken by an interdepartmental committee, which would guide the activities of the delegation and would examine its proposals (playing a role somewhat similar to that of CIAT with respect to DATAR). This would give the essential administrative projects a political dimension.[7]

The delegation would not run the risk of being confined to excessively remote, or even futuristic, activities, thanks to the permanent role that it would simultaneously have to play in the data-processing policy of the government.

It should intervene with flexibility—for example, supporting actions intended to free the consumer, such as advanced standardization, compatibility of hardware, and portability of software. It might supervise the harmonization of the interdepartmental networks with Transpac. Finally, it should contribute, perhaps as a provider of data-processing services, to assisting the departments with fewer resources to catch up with the others.

This procedure would not be accompanied by a centralization of financial resources; only a previously determined part of the "fund for administrative reform" would be allocated to data-processing interventions. This would make it possible under certain conditions to reduce the expenses of the departments in charge of the projects, conditions that would have to be determined by the government. Thus, as an example, it would be possible to contribute to agency expenses that would benefit French participants (manufacturers of large computers or paracomputer equipment and service companies). This system of bonuses would induce each agency to accept the suggestions of the delegation. It would preserve the freedom of its directors, in contrast with the present preferential policy.

The delegation should support the weaker departments. It would provide them with the data-processing experts they lack. It would assist them with its knowledge of the participants in the industry, whether manufacturers or service companies. The simplest method of intervention would consist in assigning a few data-processing specialists during the period of implementation of a large project. If such an assignment raised too many problems, the delegation might replace the weak departments in the management of the operation, acting as a provider of services.

In order to follow this policy, the delegation would need a sufficient number of technicians: to a great extent, they might be specialists already working in the administration. The increase in outside orders would certainly cause a reduction in the work load of certain data-processing services. High-level employees would thus be released, and they would be assigned to the delegation. Far from creating a corps of public data-processing specialists, whose establishment would promote rigidity, this less ambitious policy attempts to introduce flexibility in preparing for the future.

Provided that it is widespread, data processing can be in harmony with new power arrangements and even favor them.[8] Each group and each community would ensure the collection and processing of the necessary information. But far from implying a total atomization of the data-processing infrastructure, the division of responsibilities requires a solid organization of the information circuits. It requires the establishment of data banks, public or semipublic, all the more powerful as access to them will be easy and democratic and they will have to satisfy multipurpose users.[9]

There is nothing to prevent a clear distinction being made in the distant future between sovereign prerogatives exercised with all the necessary vigor and collective functions gradually transferred to peripheral bodies.

**QUESTIONS FOR THE FUTURE**

*The answer is yes, but remind me of what the
question was.*
Woody Allen

*Trend is not destiny.*
Lewis Mumford

**Introduction**

These reflections on the distant future are organized around two hypotheses:

1. In a high-productivity society, conflicts will gradually spread to all elements of social life and to all components of the cultural model, for example, language and knowledge.

2. In view of this uncertain future, what is essential is not to forecast the effects of telematics but to socialize information.

On such topics it is not necessary to reach overall conclusions but to propose a set of questions.

# WILL A COMPUTERIZED SOCIETY BE A SOCIETY OF CULTURAL CONFLICTS?

**A High-Productivity Society: A Society Beset by Conflicts**

Data processing makes possible and accelerates the rise of a very highly productive society, with less but more effective work and jobs very different from those imposed by industrial life. This change has begun: a great decrease in the labor force in the primary and secondary sectors, an increase in services, and above all a multiplication of activities in which information is the raw material.[1] It will be accompanied by a change in the structure of organizations and by fluctuations in attitudes toward work.

In France since the last war, great industrial conglomerates have grown up, governed by the law of increasing yields. For certain types of production, this will continue: it will be necessary to accept their constraints, without excessive illusions about the improvements, such as profit sharing and amenities, compatible with the discipline that is one of their intrinsic features. However, some French experience, and numerous examples abroad,[2] show that the new techniques, and especially those related to automation and data processing, can multiply the areas in which the small organization is superior to the large one in effectiveness. The social tensions, the entropy, and the vulnerability typical of over-large institutions will lead to a generalization of this spreading out of production: the workshop will replace the factory, the branch office will replace the conglomerate.[3] Gradually, therefore, industry will come to play a smaller role, and many of its installations will be split. Furthermore, the general trend of society will require a decreasing amount of productive work. In terms of total volume, this evolution is inevitable.[4]

The traditional social scene will tend to become less structured as it passes from an industrial, organic society to a polymorphous information society. Relations based on production will no longer be the single matrix of social life. Rivalries will no longer be between two classes structured by their place in the industrial process but among innumerable mobile groups, conditioned by the diversity of their membership and their projects. The source and the scope of such conflicts will extend to the entire society.

How will the confrontation between these groups distribute the tasks and the rewards of productive employment, the definition of its ends? Within a world in which the "value of work" will be eliminated, will work as value lose its importance? As a result of religious heritage and daily practice, its socializing virtues and security value have made it the cornerstone of social organization over the centuries.

Will the remaining productive activity be the duty of the reserve army of immigrants making up the lower proletariat and the prerogative of a few neurotics produced within the great incubators of technology? Will there remain a "working class" or will work, on the other hand, be distributed among a more numerous population, but one divided between a main activity providing social status and protection and a multitude of occupations devoted to forms of production outside the traditional commercial channels, to the enjoyment of leisure, or simply to social life?

Which rules, which common values will govern the inevitable coexistence of at least three forms of collective organizations: large enterprises devoted to rationalization and maximum productivity; small working units opening the way for innovation, for new products, and for new consumption, and whose law will remain aggressiveness, risk tak-

ing, and the quest for maximum profits; and public
services, cooperatives, associations, and highly
decentralized groups, with little concern about
economic and financial returns, but consumers of
labor and providers of amenities? How, within a
convivial society under the constraint of external
stability, will the subtle balance be established between two worlds as foreign to each other but also
as indispensable to each other as the nuclear world
and that of Illich?

The displacement of conflict is beginning to be
felt in most modern countries. Conflicts will continue to appear in business for a long time, but
what triggers them is gradually moving to other
areas of confrontation: the city, health, education,
and so on. The 1968 student riots were a first sign
of this transformation, which has been prolonged
by the ecological movement. The proliferation of
social life, the perception of solidarity in opposition, in neighborhood, and in leisure, show new
desires, cause new experiences, and demonstrate
the presence of tensions foreign to the world of
production. These movements are so well perceived
that current political life is a race to entice them.

Nevertheless, they are only starting the transi-
tion toward the very highly productive society,
where conflicts will predominantly be over cultural
factors and where appropriating them will become
the moving force of history.

It is then that slowly but surely telematics will
affect the major instruments of culture: language,
in its relations to the individual, and even in its
social function; and knowledge, as an extension of
collective memory and as a tool for achieving the
equality or discrimination of social groups.

**Telematics and Cultural Conflicts: Language and Knowledge[5]**

As the Sumerians were writing the first hieroglyphs on wax tablets, they were living, probably without realizing it, through a decisive change for mankind: the appearance of writing. And yet it was going to change the world. At the present time, data processing is perhaps introducing a comparable phenomenon. The analogies are striking: extension of memory; proliferation and changes in information systems; possibly a change in the models of authority. The astonishing similarities may be far-fetched. The importance of this transformation, however, remains incomprehensible to those who live through it, unless it is considered from the viewpoint of Fabrice at Waterloo.

Even a method is lacking: if data processing in the long run produces a decisive change in language and in knowledge, it will involve changes in thinking, in concepts, and in reasoning, which will slowly obliterate the tools used to forecast them. What to do—to ask questions that have no answers and give answers only in order to raise new questions?

**Telematics, Language, and Dominance**

The enormous spread of data processing that will occur when access vocabulary is standardized will affect language and syntax. By penetrating into the activities based on communication (office work, preparation of legal instruments, composition of texts, and so on), telematics resorts to an apparently vehicular language that actually is of a different nature, because it is modular.

As an example of things to come, office data processing attempts to reproduce dialogues in a manner strictly limited to its requirements and is inventing a simplified language in order to communicate at minimum cost. This evolution will prevail over the years: it combines ease and effectiveness by sacrificing part of the content, to which intellectuals are more sensitive than managers.

In the first period, this application of data processing to writing will affect the texts that are poorest in "signifiers." This will not be a major change in relation to a mode of writing that is already repetitive and mechanical. But beyond that? Where will processed communication stop, when households begin to be equipped with computers? This question might appear to be unwarranted without the precedent of electronic calculators. Fifteen years ago, nobody would have imagined the proliferation of cheap devices available to everybody and especially to students. Today, the question is no longer whether mental calculation is going to become less important but when it is going to disappear.

What will traditional writing become when a processed language, a poorer one but one sufficient to express the essential meaning of messages related to daily life, becomes available to everybody? Language translates and generates a method of organization: to touch it is to shake society itself. In effect, it produces and reproduces the social hierarchy; certainly, the speech of the lower classes is now more remote from that of the dominant classes than their respective lifestyles. Cultural inequality is by now predominant, and language plays a major role in it. Will the general adoption of processed language favor emancipation or will it emphasize the differences? It will not affect each user equally. Doubtless, it will not stop being improved and will become capable of more and more elaborate dialogues. But its propagation among the different social classes will not be uniform: they will not show equal resistance to the introduction of a codified and abbreviated language. Their permeability will depend upon their cultural level, and since the latter is not similar, telematics will have a discriminatory effect. More than ever, language will become a stake of culture. Opposing groups will struggle to appropriate it.

Telematics, Knowledge, and Power

The cultural model of a society also depends on its memory, control of which largely conditions the hierarchy of power. Access to infinitely greater sources of information will entail basic changes and will affect the social structure by modifying the procedures for acquiring knowledge.

With telematics, the storage of information changes in size and in nature. Storage in computers requires an organizational effort, based on both technical constraints and financial imperatives. The establishment of data banks is going to be the beginning of a rapid restructuring of knowledge, following patterns that now are difficult to define. The change will take place on the initiative of the sponsors of such banks, most probably in the United States. Therefore, criteria originating from the American cultural model will prevail.

Thus data processing runs the risk of being at the source of one of those discontinuities around which knowledge revolves. The boundaries of disciplines will be more fluid, more mobile, because they will be the result of multiple codifications, of scattered endeavors without direction or design. Related primarily to the nature of data banks, this evolution will thus reflect the influence of American culture, which is not organized into battle corps and does not establish guilds. The multiplication of configurations will reduce the importance of unifying classifications; knowledge will then lose the comforting support of a tradition and of a sociology. Will it gain an ounce of freedom from it?

Data processing will also revolutionize an individual culture that mainly consists in the accumulation of exact knowledge. Discrimination will then be based less on the storage of knowledge than on the ability to research and use it. Concepts will prevail over facts, iteration over recitation. Accepting this transformation will constitute a Copernican revolution for pedagogy. The priority given to the acquisition of a universal microknowledge is now related to a concept of culture whose permanence is ensured by the school. This is inseparable from the sociological features of the world of schools and universities, of the special merit system on which it is based, and of the ideology that prevails among the teachers. This oscillation toward learning structures and concepts will certainly take place slowly. It will open with a period in which teaching will not yet be adjusted to the metamorphosis represented by the data banks. During that period, children, for whom the school is the principal cultural mold, will be defenseless before this new approach to knowledge.

All changes in knowledge are accompanied by social changes. The rise of the middle class was simultaneous with that of the book, the appearance of the technocratic classes with the development of economics, sociology, and psychology; that is, the new disciplines that enriched the methods by which power could be exercised. The telematics revolution will have consequences that cannot be evaluated at the present time. One should have to have a very static concept of social change to regard it as a "game of goose" in which one group retreats a few steps and another group advances by a few steps known in advance.

# PLANNING FOR AN UNCERTAIN FUTURE: SOCIALIZING INFORMATION

**An Uncertain Future**

If the first hypothesis is correct, the future becomes unforeseeable. The liberal and Marxist approaches, contemporaries of the production-based society, are rendered questionable by its demise.[1]

The liberal approach tends to confuse history with economic laws. It only considers conflicts in terms of the market and tends to return them to this field if they escape. Thus management aims at limiting the field of ideology and at expanding that of the market. Politics—insofar as it deals with the perception and handling of struggles for power —is apparently rejected. Actually, it is conjured away: it becomes less the field of deliberate and explicit action than the field of what is left unsaid. The vision of the future ends with a tranquilized postindustrial society. It assumes that affluence and the growing equality of standards of living will make it possible to build the nation around an immense culturally homogeneous middle class, and to overcome tensions.

The Marxist analysis recognizes conflicts, but it relates their evolution to the single opposition between two classes organized by relations of production. Arising from the suffering of the primitive accumulation of capital, it rests upon a simplistic, all-encompassing, and rigid view of power relationships, incapable of integrating the increasing complexity of modern societies. It is not surprising that the goal of history, arrival of the classless society, is reached quite simply by the collective appropriation of the means of production. It is a vision at least as mystifying as the postindustrial society.

The information society does not fit these analyses and predictions. Going beyond the world of production, it fashions its new requirements according to its own plan, its own regulatory pat-

terns, and its own cultural model. It is the locus of
an infinite number of decentralized, unexpressed
conflicts that do not respond to a unifying analysis.
Certainly, the systems approach can better explain
a multipolar society, but the latter can have no a
priori strategy. Even its values will be the subject
of multiple rivalries, and the results will be uncertain—it will be an uncertain society. The longer
history continues, the more people make it, and
the less they know what history they are fashioning.

Thus the future no longer depends on the approach but on the quality of the collective plan
and on the nature of the regulations on which it
is based.

**Until Now: Regulation**
**without Plan, Plan**
**without Regulation**

Liberalism produces mercantile societies: it is a
system of regulation without a plan. Marxist management creates—but it is not the only one—protective societies: they constitute plans without regulation. Both reduce society to the level of the poor
information on which they are based.

In the liberal world, competition and its result,
the price system, play the roles of both information and decision. They assure, for better or for
worse, the adjustment of individual plans capable
of solution. The entire society is measured by the
single standard of commercial value; the market
becomes the only "overall" value of society, and
the supreme judge of values.

This view has the advantage of offering an ap-
proximate guideline for interpretation and action,
insofar as it is applied to the flows of information
governing the behavior of producers and consumers. But it is useless in confronting what goes
beyond commercial activities, that which depends
on the cultural model, on the "formative matrix."

The constraints arising from long-term strategies, which exceed the strength and the stakes of individuals and of groups, are layered. The hierarchy of individual or collective choices cannot be discussed *ex ante*. Its *ex post* implementation will never be the sum total of preferences but an adjustment suffered unevenly. In such a system, each individual can only measure the unfulfilled part of his initial desire and blame the others for his unfulfillment. No mechanism of political participation can compensate for the resulting feeling of alienation and frustration.

Marxist management, as practiced in the Eastern countries, is led to regard "indoctrination-information" as a tool for bringing reality within an imaginary framework, for reducing society to its ideological model. It tends to create protective systems and for that purpose only needs information from below. Information from above will be in the form of orders. The intention is not to take into account decentralized plans but to give to each group and to each individual its allotted role in the implementation of the collective plan.

All regulation by decree seeks integration by a mystical participation. Sometimes, it can be obtained. Starting from the statement that the "principal plan of the center" ontologically and in the long run expresses the collective essence of individual desires, it justifies its present difficulties by its historical purposes and attempts to establish a system of representation that creates an emotional link between the collective plan and individual behavior.

The weakness of such a system rests upon its internal contradiction. Civil society does not speak. Its only expression lies in the gaps, in the interstices. Thus the logic of the center tends to drift away from reality. Having, on principle, suffocated the expression of desires and needs (even prices are no longer barometers but commands), the information from below, needed by the center to establish its plan, becomes only the mirror image of its own desire. By insisting upon erasing the signals and information that might be transmitted by the many facets of real society, the "apparatchiks" only manage the nightmares of their fellow citizens, their own dreams, or their own interests.

In a highly productive society, rich and well-distributed information must be able to make the spontaneity of social groups and the inevitable burden of constraints compatible.

**Socializing Information**

In an ideal world of fully informed "wise men," organization would coincide with spontaneity: a perfect market society, in which education and information would make each person conscious of the collective constraints, and a fully planned society, in which the center would receive from each unit at the base correct messages concerning its order of preferences and would have the same structure and the same attitude. Information and participation advance together.

As long as it is up to citizens to express their quantifiable desires and up to the public authorities to perform their short-term regulatory activities, the market remains an effective forum for confrontations.

But the groups' plans are increasingly expressing social and cultural aspirations. Simultaneously, external pressures will increase. Public authorities must preserve the future of society: the great disruptions in the international division of labor will require decisions by the government. Decentralized indicators and spontaneous reactions will not make it possible to prepare for massive scarcities, which can be forecast in the long run but which are only barely hinted at by current prices. Similarly, no individual forecast will determine the limit of national sovereignty beyond which all freedom of choice for the community will disappear. Only an authority possessing the appropriate information can promote development and guarantee the independence of the country: it is the mediator of vital constraints.

A smooth functioning of society requires that social groups be able to express their aspirations and their dislikes, but that at the same time information concerning the constraints be received and accepted. There is no spontaneity without regulation and no regulation without a hierarchical system. A self-managed and self-sufficient society will remain marginally dissident. In order to contribute to the transformation of the entire society, it must accept a strategy of participation.

Therefore socializing information means establishing the mechanisms whereby constraints and freedoms, the prerogative plan and the aspirations of independent groups, are managed and harmonized. It means promoting the preparation of data on the basis of which the strategy of the center and the desires of the periphery may reach agreement whereby Society and the State not only support each other but produce each other.

In order to do so, however, it is necessary to eliminate a basic contradiction: if information appears at the level of the decentralized units, it cannot be used as such for most of their decisions. It assumes its significance only through syntheses in which it confronts the long-term difficulties and the collective plan. It must then be returned in

such a form that it will spontaneously produce
correct reactions. This requires it to appear legitimate and effective, and its circulation must be
institutionalized.

The British say that a fact must be respected like
the "lord mayor." But what would be the weight
of this dictum in a country in which the legitimacy
of the lords mayor is contested? Legitimacy is the
result of the procedure whereby they are ap-
pointed: all those who will be subjected to their
authority participate in it. At present, information
from above is not well received because it is
resented as an extension of power, as a manipulation; it will be increasingly necessary to call its
recipients to participate in its preparation, so that
the recipients are also the transmitters and the
transmissions take conditions for receiving into account. This participation will only be accepted if
rival groups are equally capable of producing, processing, and transmitting their own information.
This requires that most citizens be able to form
communities or associations, public or private, and
equip themselves to collect and use the information that justifies their plans.

But what type of information is involved? The
people in charge will have to establish properly
arranged sets of factual data, showing the constraints of the government, the purpose of the
collective project, and whether it constitutes a
plan or not. Effectiveness requires that the data be
prepared by cross-examination, that their format
render them easy to transmit, and that easy access
make it possible to criticize them. It is not sufficient for them to be generally accepted as objective. Each group must also be able, on the basis of
the same constraints, to reach an original reconcili-

ation with its own projects, and the debate must produce alternative solutions. This requires that information can be exchanged with others and that it take into account environmental constraints, those resulting from the objectives of other groups and those arising from the common center, the public authorities.

Information that only teaches technical solutions, that lists facts without putting them into a perspective and without structuring them into a coherent project, and, on the other hand, information that proclaims ideals without inserting them into the practical development of society will increasingly be regarded as pseudo-information. Making information useful, therefore, means reaching a minimum agreement on the structure that transforms it into coherent and accepted thought.[2]

Furthermore, the resulting project must be inserted within a system of communications and concerted action. At the present time, information basically goes from the top to the bottom. Only the market constitutes a network, and a poor one, for horizontal communication. The information society requires focusing on the center of the desires of the independent groups and an unlimited multiplication of lateral communications.

This must make it possible to compare formalized items of information to reveal those projects deriving from the base that exceed the quantified data from the market. The massive computerization of society will have to be utilized to create this new "network," in which each homogeneous community will be able to communicate with its counterparts and with the center. Oral communication, with its rituals, gave the village its stability. Processed communication, and its codes, must re-

create an "informational agora" expanded to the
size of the modern nation. Thus agreements and
compromises will gradually be reached. They will
express a consensus involving ever larger communities, and increasingly long-range views.

Stability in a computerized society is difficult to
achieve. In outline, national life will be organized
at three levels, corresponding to three functions,
to three regulatory systems, and therefore to three
information systems. The sovereign state itself is
where the collective plan will be established; the
public authorities will determine the relative importance of the constraints to which society is subjected. They may use the market, but they must
not retreat before a direct command or direct
control. Here, regulation is essentially based on
political mechanisms. The stage at which social
and cultural programs will be organized and confront one another will be the field of the "informational agora." The market stage, based on the price
system, will be where the spontaneous desires of
groups are expressed and decided, insofar as they
concern marketable goods and are quantifiable.
Actually, these stages will interfere: as the constraints imposed by the common interest and by
cultural aspirations are better expressed, they will
tend to affect the market. The latter may stop
being a metaphysical entity and become a tool. It
will reflect exchange values increasingly dominated
by motivations that go beyond them. It will be a
quasi-market, which will recover a temporal scope
and a range of desires that until then will have
eluded it.

This dynamic, in which each regulatory system is
enriched by the information originating from the
other two, is the royal road that could be followed
by a country that has generalized communication

and thereby expanded participation. But the
society that it produces is fragile; built to favor the
formation of a consensus, it presupposes its existence and it is blocked if it cannot obtain it. Excessive or poorly accepted constraints would only
enable it to recover its stability by an increase in
authoritarianism. An irresponsible promotion of
social and cultural aspirations, incompatible with
the constraints, would reduce the collective plan
to its proper size or would cause a strong reaction
on the part of the advocates of sovereign power.
This would be a prelude to a compromise in favor
of checking the movement of history.

In order to make the information society possible, it is necessary to have knowledge but also to
have time. The reciprocal learning process of disciplines and aspirations takes place slowly: it
operates through the generations, by transforming
cultural patterns—families, universities, media, and
so on.

Data processing has falsely crystallized our concerns. They rise again, more general and stronger,
at the end of this analysis. Will the urgency and
scope of the constraints to which French society
will be subjected grant it the time required for this
vital learning process?

# SUMMARY OF THE APPENDIXES*

**Volume 1**
**New Data Processing and New Growth**

**Appendix 1**

**Network Systems, Telecommunications, and Telematics**

To a great extent, networks are the source of the turning point in data processing; the appendix defines their place in telecommunications. Technical progress and the appearance of telematics require a rationalization whose procedures are studied in this document.

More specifically, it deals with Transpac and satellites and provides information concerning telecommunications and networks in the principal industrialized countries.

**Appendix 2**

**Data Banks**

Telematics will make the development of data banks possible. Economic data banks in particular will be increasingly important. The appendix studies the situations and policies of some large countries in these fields.

**Appendix 3**

**Data Processing and Macroeconomics: An Initial Approach**

By the increased productivity that it generates, the data-processing turning point affects the macroeconomic equilibrium. The appendix fits those effects within the framework of the basic trends of the French economy and describes the difficulties analysis faces, for lack of appropriate tools.

*The full text of the appendixes, in three volumes, and the supporting documents summarized in the following section, will be published by Editione du Seuil (La Documentation Française).

Appendix 4                    **The Information Society and New Growth: A
                              Study of Some Foreign Approaches (Japan,
                              American Research)**
                              The Japanese Jacudi Report is an attempt to com·
                              prehend the future of a computerized society.
                              From a different viewpoint, studies have been
                              carried out in the United States in order to define
                              "the information economy." The appendix pre-
                              sents these two initiatives, describes their contri-
                              butions, and outlines their limitations.

                              **Volume 2
                              The Data-Processing Industry and Data-Processing
                              Services**

Appendix 5                    **An Approach to an Economic Evaluation of the
                              Uses of Data Processing**
                              It is difficult to evaluate quantitatively the effects
                              of data processing on the macroeconomic equi-
                              librium, for theoretical and practical reasons that
                              are outlined in this document. It describes the
                              studies that should be undertaken.

Appendix 6                    **The Computerization of Society: Analytical
                              Structures in Some Foreign Countries**
                              The data-processing turning point, the appearance
                              of telematics, and the evolution of telecommunica-
                              tions have been studied abroad. The appendix
                              describes the means adopted by governments to
                              consider such questions.

Appendix 7                    **The Data-Processing Industry (Its Development,
                              Its Policies, and Its Situation in Various Countries)**
                              This appendix presents a balance sheet of the data-
                              processing industry in France, in the United
                              States, in Japan, in the Federal Republic of

Germany, and in Great Britain. It points out the advantages of each country to approach the era of remote data processing on an industrial scale.

**Appendix 8**

**Evolution of the Data-Processing Hardware Market from 1976 to 1980**
This appendix provides quantified information concerning the probable evolution of data-processing applications by sectors of the economy.

**Appendix 9**

**Service and Data-Processing Consulting Companies (SSCI)**
The French SSCI have developed to a remarkable extent. They now constitute an important element in a new data-processing strategy. The appendix analyzes their situation and their possible evolution.

**Appendix 10**

**Data Processing and French Government Administration**
The administration has undergone a rapid computerization for which the appendix draws up a balance sheet. The future of administrative data processing can only be conceived in the light of a study of the evolution of the administration itself: it is in this spirit that new structures might find a place.

Several supplementary notes complete this analysis: they concern data processing in Social Security, in the budget office, in the Direction Générale des Impôts (taxes), and procurement, as well as the administrative data pilot operation (OPIDA) and the ENEIDE data bank.

**Appendix 11**

**Internal Data-Processing Departments**
Traditional data processing has remained a prerogative of large organizations and of their data-

processing departments. The latter are going to evolve as a result of the telematics transformation. Their role, their status, and their policies must change.

**Volume 3**
**The New Data Processing and Its User (Business and Government Administration)**

Appendix 12

**Small and Intermediate Users (MPU)**
The development of low-cost and powerful data processing will entail the appearance of thousands of users: small and medium-sized companies pro- fessionals, and businessmen. This "democratiza- tion," as the appendix shows, will not take place everywhere at the same rate and in the same manner.

# SUMMARY OF THE SUPPORTING DOCUMENTS

**Volume 4**

**Supporting Document no. 1**
**The Turning Point in Data Processing**
This document traces a history of the changes in data processing—the evolution of hardware and software. From this viewpoint, it examines current changes: the development of small-scale data processing and the appearance of networks.

**Supporting Document no. 2**
**Evolution of the Performance and the Performance/Price Ratio of Hardware and Software**
Also analyzing the major stages in the history of data processing, this document basically concentrates on improvements in the production of software, which is gradually becoming an industry.

**Supporting Document no. 3**
**What Happened to Life Patterns? (Reflections on the Canadian Experience with Computerization)**
Canada was the first country conscious of the osmosis of data processing and telecommunications. It has adopted a telematics policy. The document examines the main directions of this strategy and, with the benefit of hindsight, raises questions about that experience.

**Supporting Document no. 4**
**The Introduction of Data Processing in Medicine and Health**
The document analyzes the overall effects of data processing on medicine, its use for diagnostic purposes, changes in medical practice, evolution of the relations between specialists and general practitioners, between general practitioners and auxiliary health personnel, and so on. Finally, it

defines the conditions that should favor the computerization of medicine.

### Supporting Document no. 5
### Legal Problems of Computerization

The document deals with the large legal problems raised by computerization. They concern first of all the preservation of individual liberties but also questions concerning the relations between the data-processing profession and its users, as well as the difficulties raised by the specific nature of the data-processing "object."

### Supporting Document no. 6
### Data Processing and Local Power

Data processing alters the balance between the state and local communities, and among the communities themselves. The document analyzes the areas in which such phenomena appear, how they operate, and the possibility of using them for decentralization purposes.

### Supporting Document no. 7
### Taking into Account Working Conditions in Decisions Concerning the Automation of Administration

Data processing alters working conditions, often improving them, sometimes worsening them. This document attempts to draw up a brief balance sheet of those effects and then specifies how the managers of data-processing projects might consider them in the design of systems.

### Supporting Document no. 8
### Information Research and Technology

Data processing is diversifying and multiplying its fields of application, which should stimulate

research. The document describes the role that the
IRIA play in this effort.

### Supporting Document no. 9
### Data Processing and Its Image
Data processing is the source of many myths.
In addition to a theoretical approach to this
phenomenon, the document analyzes the
image of data processing appearing in the press
and outlines a series of surveys.

### Supporting Document no. 10
### Advanced Applications of Computerization
Some applications of data processing appear to be
particularly innovative. They are still either at the
experimental stage or in limited use. The document describes about ten of them, showing their
use, their field of application, and their possible
effects.

# ACKNOWLEDGMENTS

This report is the sole responsibility of its two authors. Nevertheless, it has benefited from a great volume of contributions and assistance.

In some cases officials in the administration and the private sector have opened their agencies and their companies to us. They themselves, along with their most highly qualified collaborators in the fields of data processing and telecommunications, have enabled us to profit from their experience.

In other cases particularly competent people have accepted the heavy task of preparing the appendixes and supporting documents. Most often, they have benefited from the aid of working groups or from personal assistance.

Finally, this report would not be what it is if we had not been able to rely on previous studies dealing with data processing and with society. We especially want to mention those by Maurice Allègre, Jacques Attali, Michel Crozier, Michel Foucault, Robert Lattes, Jacques Lesourne, Pierre Lhermitte, Bruno Lussato, Edgar Morin, Joel de Rosnay, François Sarda, Bertrand Schwartz, Michel Serres, Alain Touraine, and Bernard Tricot. Some of them have kindly provided us with oral or written suggestions.

We also thank the following:

## 1. Institutions and their executives

• The Computerization of Society Commission of the Ministry of Industry. Under the leadership of Alain Taib, that body has effectively supported our research. Alain Taib and Philippe Lemoine, in addition to the specific studies they carried out, which are mentioned later, have also participated in our discussions.

• The electronic and data-processing industries administration of the Ministry of Industry, and especially its director, Jean-Claude Pelissolo.

• The general telecommunications administration (DGT), and particularly Gérard Théry, director general for telecommunications, and Philippe Picard, assistant director in charge of remote data processing.

• The office of the state secretary for postal service and telecommunications, particularly Hervé Nora.

• Télé-Diffusion de France, particularly Jean Autin, president, and Maurice Remy, director-general.

• The National Center for Space Studies, particularly its director, Yves Sillard.

• The presidents of the ministerial commissions for data processing.

• CII–Honeywell Bull, particularly Jean-Pierre Brule, president, Jean Gaudfernau, secretary-general, and Emmanuel de Robien, who arranged our contacts with his company.

• IBM France, particularly Jacques Maisonrouge, president of IBM World Trade, Jacques Herbart, former president of IBM France, Jacques Lemonnier, president of IBM France, and Claude Andreuzza, who arranged our contacts with his company.

• SYNTEC, syndicate of data-processing service and consulting companies, CIGREF, data-processing club of large French enterprises, and INFOREP, data-processing distribution association.

2. The reporters and the working groups who prepared the appendixes

• Appendix 1, "Network Systems, Telecommunications, and Telematics," was prepared by Jacques

Pomonti and Jean-François David of ICS Conseils.
It was based on the work of a group including
Hervé Nora and Picard, as well as Mr. Schoeller,
regional director of telecommunications at Mont-
pellier, and Mr. Voge, director in charge of inter-
national relations at the National Telecommuni-
cations Research Center. It was submitted to DGT,
DIELI, TDF, CNES, IRIA, CII-HB, and to IBM
France. It has largely heeded the advice provided
by those bodies.
• Appendix 2, "Data Banks," was prepared by
Raimundo Beca, head of the Computerization of
Society Commission of the Ministry of Industry.
It was based on the work of a group that included
Messrs. Arditi, Eksl, and Marre, all from the Geste
Company, and Mr. Joyeux of the Computerization
of Society Commission. The group also benefited
from the collaboration and support of Mr. Buffet
from CNES, Mrs. Morin and Messrs. Michel and
Chambaud from ENIST, Mr. Labin, consultant
to BNIST, Mrs. Moreau, French Petroleum Institute, and Mr. Salmona, director of OPIDA, as well
as Messrs. Treille from CESA and Repesford from
the statistical bureau of the United Nations.
• Appendix 3, "Data Processing and Macroeconomics," was prepared by Frédéric Saint-
Geours, civil administrator of the Ministry of
Economics and Finance. It is based on the work of
a group that included Messrs. Alidieres, chief of
the Division of Planning Coordination in the Forecasting Department, Bonnet, permanent scientific
adviser to IRIA, Froment, technical adviser to the
Forecasting Office, Lemoine, head of the Computerization of Society Commission, Lenclud,
chief of the Data-Processing Division of the Forecasting Department, Mignot, chief of the Program
Service of INSEE, Sicherman, administrator of

INSEE, Taib, chief of the Computerization of Society Commission, and Virol, head of the office of the general commissioner for planning. The group read the text of the appendix and approved it.

• Appendix 4, "The Information Society and New Growth: A Study of Some Foreign Approaches (Japan, American Research)," was prepared by Philippe Lemoine, head of the Computerization of Society Commission, who benefited from the studies by Messrs. Bonnet and Sautter for the analysis dealing with Japan. The text was reread and approved by the group mentioned in connection with appendix 3.

• Appendix 5, "An Approach to an Economic Evaluation of the Uses of Data Processing," was prepared by Georges Sicherman, administrator of INSEE.

• Appendix 6, "The Computerization of Society: Analytical Structures in Some Foreign Countries," was prepared by Berthe Favier, who also coordinated the entire project.

• Appendix 7, "The Data-Processing Industry (Its Development, Its Policies, and Its Situation in Various Countries)," was prepared by Messrs. Jean-Marie Fabre and Thierry Moulonguet. It was submitted to DIELI, CII-HB, and IBM. The suggestions made by them have enriched our thoughts on the subject.

• Appendix 8, "Evolution of the Data-Processing Hardware Market from 1976 to 1980," was prepared by Jean-Marie Fabre and Thierry Moulonguet after consultation with manufacturers.

• Appendix 9, "Service and Data-Processing Consulting Companies," was prepared by Francis Bacon, member of the Computerization of Society Commission, and Jacques Pomonti and Jean-Francois David from ICS Conseils. It was the sub-

ject of a broad discussion, involving Messrs. Carteron, president of STERIA, Dorleac, president of TSIL, Dreyfus, vice-president of CAP-SOGETI, Joseph, general manager of SERTI, Kampf, president of CAP-SOGETI, Nollet, president of CISI, Sahut d'Izarn, president of CERCI, Saint-Geours, president of SEMA, Schlumberger, president of SERTI, Stern, president of SESA, and Thellier, general manager of ECA Automation. Their suggestions, as well as those of the bodies to which this appendix was submitted, DIELI, CII-HB, and IBM France, have guided most of our conclusions.
• Appendix 10, "Data Processing and French Government Administration," was prepared by Philippe Jaffré, inspector of finances, on the basis of the work of a group that included Messrs. Baquiast, assistant director of customs, Empereur, assistant director of taxation, Salmona, director of the OPIDA Project, Vidal, technical adviser to the taxation administration, Coiffard, administrator of INSEE, Callot, member of the Commission for the Promotion of Data Processing of the Ministry of Industry, Taib, member of the Computerization of Society Commission, and Beca, also a member of the Computerization of Society Commission. Additional collaborators were Miss Le Laurier and Messrs. Gourdon, Lamy, Madec, and Théron, as well as Messrs. Beer-Gabel, Brochard, Callies, Coulas, Fontaniel, Gibert, Haas, Léger, Poupon, Seibel, and Zeitoun.
• Appendix 11, "Internal Data-Processing Departments," was prepared by Alain Taib, member of the Computerization of Society Commission. It was submitted for advice to Messrs. Alba, former vice-president of CIGREF, in charge of data processing for the ELF-Aquitaine group, Pelletier, secretary-general of CIGREF, and Empereur, president

of INFOREP and assistant director of the taxation administration.

• Appendix 12, "Small and Intermediate Users," was prepared by Joel Baur, member of the Computerization of Society Commission. It was prepared on the basis of surveys and working meetings with both manufacturers and users. It benefited from assistance by Messrs. Audoin, Bertin, and David, as well as Mrs. Paré and Messrs. Ballerin, Barbe, Berty, Bonamy, Bret, Claret, Dalloz, Demians, Ducrocq, Hayat, Paps, and Rochet.

• The bibliography was compiled by Isabelle Félix, member of the Computerization of Society Commission, who benefited from assistance by Mr. Grandperret, head of research and teaching at CEPIA, as well as by Mrs. Raoul-Duval and Mr. Lemoine.

3. The authors and working groups who prepared the supporting documents

• Supporting Document no. 1, "The Turning Point in Data Processing," was prepared by Raymond Moch, honorary assistant director at Collège de France.

• Supporting Document no. 2, "Evolution of the Performance and the Performance/Price Ratio of Hardware and Software," was prepared by Xavier Dalloz, member of the Computerization of Society Commission of the Ministry of Industry.

• Supporting Document no. 3, "What Happened to Life Patterns?," was prepared by Philippe Lemoine, member of the Computerization of Society Commission.

• Supporting Document no. 4, "The Introduction of Data Processing in Medicine and Health," was prepared by Prof. Funck-Brentano on the basis of the work of a group that included Mr. Akoun, chief of the medical data-processing section of DOMI in the Department of Health, Prof. Bricaud, Col. Crocq, Mr. Forge, director of CXP, Dr. Joly, Mr. Joyeux, member of the Computerization of Society Commission, Prof. Laudat, Prof. Laurent, Mr. Mathiot, director of SETI in the Paris public welfare department. Jean Weber, former technical adviser to the Office of the Minister of Health, facilitated the organization of the working group.

• Supporting Document no. 5, "Legal Problems of Computerization," was prepared by Philippe Lemoine, member of the Computerization of Society Commission, on the basis of the work of a group that included Mr. Chamoux, an engineer-consultant, Mr. Joinet, chancery magistrate, Mrs. de Lamberterie from CNRS, and Miss Trebucq, magistrate. Bernard Tricot of the Council of State, general reporter of the Commission on Data Processing and Freedom, kindly examined this document and approved it insofar as the parts dealing with data processing and freedom are concerned.

• Supporting Document no. 6, "Data Processing and Local Power," was prepared by Bertrand Eveno, inspector of finance and fomer reporter to the Commission for the Development of Local Responsibilities presided over by Olivier Guichard.

• Supporting Document no. 7, "Taking into Account Working Conditions in Decisions Concerning the Automation of Administration," was prepared by Gérard Rolloy, member of ANACT

• Supporting Document no. 8, "Information Research and Technology," was prepared by André Danzin, director of IRIA.

• Supporting Document no. 9, "Data Processing and Its Image," was prepared by Philippe Lemoine, member of the Computerization of

Society Commission, on the basis of the studies carried out by Messrs. Marie, Masson, Mathieu, Ollivier, Ricard, and Weis of the Center for Sociological Studies and Applied Research Studies, as well as by Mrs. Ennel and Mrs. Gallouedec-Genuys of the French Institute of Administrative Sciences.
• Supporting Document no. 10, "Advanced Applications of Computerization," was prepared by Louis Joyeux, member of the Computerization of Society Commission, in collaboration with Messrs. Beca, Lemoine, and Taib of the same commission. They received assistance from the following individuals: Mr. Crémieux-Brilhac, director of Documentation Française, Mr. Coiffard from UTA, Messrs. Couzy and de Montricher from OPIT, Messrs. Dentaud and Dandelot from the Bank of France, Mr. Dreyfous of Air France, Mr. Gouesfon, technical adviser to the Office of the Secretary of State for Tourism, Messrs. Kock and Lafond from the Ministry of Education, Mr. Leddet of the Ministry of Procurement, Mr. Michel, permanent secretary of BNIST, Mr. Motard from CNET, Mr. Termens from the DGT, and Mr. Touzelet, secretary-general of SIMPRO-FRANCE, as well as Messr. Cochet, Jeantet, Rainsard, and Richard from CERCI and Messrs. Amyel, Hellenis, Le Guillou, Ponthus, Poulaillon, Renaud, Sarrazin, and Vivier, from CAP-SOGETI.

4. In addition to these who participated in the working groups, we wish to thank the following officials of the French administration:

Mr. Chaigneau, director of ANACT, Mr. Conruyt, director of CCETT, Mr. Coursier, director of GEPI, Mr. Dondoux, general engineer for telecommunications, Mr. Engepand, director-general of industry,

Mr. Essig, delegate for land management and regional action, Mr. Jacque, professor at the University of Legal, Political, Social, and Technological Sciences of Strasbourg, Mr. de L'Estoile, former director-general of industry, Mr. Libois, chief counselor of the court of audits, former director-general of telecommunications, Mr. Oudin, delegate to PMI, Mr. Ripert, former general commissioner for procurement and productivity planning, and Mr. Souviron, director of industrial and international affairs at the DGT.

Also, Mr. Ayrault, chief of GCCIIA at DIELI, Mr. Bonafi, assistant director for public accounting, Mr. Breau of DATAR, Mr. Brochier, civil administrator in the Office of the Budget Director, Mrs. Chaumont of DATAR, Mr. Couraud, of the personnel administration of the Ministry of Procurement, Mr. Dhombres, scientific adviser to the French Embassy in Ottawa, Mr. Guinet, associate director of CCETT, Mr. Jung, scientific attaché of the French Embassy in Washington, D.C., Mr. Kaiser, scientific attaché of the French Embassy in Bonn, Mr. Kaufmant, president of the Institute for the Management of Information, Mr. Lafay, department head at GEPI, Mr. Paré of DIELI, Mr. Stourdze from IRIS, Mr. Vicarini, former member of the Data Processing Commission in the Ministry of Industry, and Mr. Vicariot, scientific adviser to the French Embassy in London.

5. We also thank the following members of international and foreign institutions:

Mr. Bernasconi, director-general of IBI, Mr. Costa, principal assistant to the director-general of IBI, Mr. Dordick, associate director of the Annenberg School of Communications, Mr. Garric, chief of

the data-processing division of the general administration for industrial and technological affairs of
the EEC, Mr. Gassmann, chief of the information,
data processing, and communications unit of the
administration for science, technology, and industry of the OECD, Mr. Kimbel of the administration for scientific affairs of OECD, Mr. Layton,
director of the general administration for internal
marketing and industrial affairs of the EEC, Mr.
Mrozinski, executive secretary of the Committee
on Telecommunications, National Research Council, Mr. Riotte, of the data-processing division of
the general administration for industrial and technological affairs of the EEC, and Mr. Valentin, of
the aeronautical division of the same administration.

6. We thank the following company officials:

Mr. Amouyal, director-general of CISI, Mr.
Audibert, president and director-general of
ALVAN, Mr. Barré, former president of CII, Mr.
Bonelli, director-general of SEMA, Mr. Bounine,
vice-president of AMI, Mr. Dautresme, director at
the central office of Crédit Lyonnais, Mr. Edeline,
president and director-general of SEP, Mr. Esteva,
general manager of Union des Assurances de Paris,
Mr. Fauroux, president and director-general of
Saint-Gobain Industries, Mr. Gelinier, director-
general of CEGOS, Mr. Lallement, director-general
of Caisse Nationale de Crédit Agricole, Mr. Maillet,
president of Intertechnique, Mr. Plescoff, president of Assurances Générales de France, Mr. Seban,
president of the Club de la Péri-Informatique, and
Mr. Vernier-Palliez, president and director-general
of Régie Nationale des Usines Renault.

Finally, we thank Mr. Barberis of Crédit Lyonnais, Mr. Benabes of Esso, Mr. Bouchaud of Saint-Gobain Industries, Mr. Bruno of CIGREF, Mr. de Carbonnel of Boston Consulting Group, Mr. Chauche, sociologist, Mr. Demeure of Rhone-Poulenc, Mr. Desor of SNCF, Mr. Dirol of Caisses des Dépots et Consignations, Mr. Eelsen of Régie Nationale des Usines Renault, Mr. d'Erceville of Péchiney-Ugine-Khulmann, Mr. Garric of Point, Mr. Soly of Caisse Nationale de Crédit Agricole, Mr. Lejart of Union des Assurances de Paris, Mr. Lepidi of Charbonnages de France, Miss Leventer of Point, Mr. Mouly of Saint-Gobain Industries, Mr. Pecqueraux of La Redoute, Mr. Petitzon of Shell, Mr. Raimond of Banque Régionale d'Escompte et de Dépots, Mr. Rameille of Régie Nationale des Usines Renault, Mr. de Russe of Société Générale, Mr. Thibadeau of Assurances Générales de France, and Mr. Vidal of SEP.

# GLOSSARY

**Access Procedure**

In a data transmission network, it is necessary to harmonize the messages from the different computers if they are to exchange information.

The access procedure, based on conventions established during the design of the network, assures the transmission and reception of messages by checking their editing, managing their control characters, and validating them.

Related terms: Connection Procedure, Networks.

**Analog Transmission**

Transmission of signals that vary continuously between two states and represent either a physical magnitude or a mathematical variable.

An example of analog transmission is the transmission of speech by telephone.

Related term: Digital Transmission.

**Antiope**

A new system developed in France by CCETT, aiming at individual remote data processing.

It comprises a central station, which memorizes the information, arranges it into pages, and transmits it, a wide-band (television) broadcasting network, and, finally, a page-selection mechanism connected to the network and combined with the user's television receiver.

It allows the cyclical transmission of pages of information, some of which are selected and displayed on the user's television screen.

Related term: Networks.

**Assembler**

A symbolic programing language, each one of whose instructions corresponds to one of the instructions in the machine language of a computer.

Prepared by Mrs. Claire-Liliane Gaudfernau, Scientific Adviser to the Coordinator for Measurements and Data Processing of ONERA, and by Mr. Alain Taib, Chief of the Mission on Data Processing and Society.

The purpose of the assembler instructions is to act as a mnemonic code for one or possibly several machine instructions.

The translation program that establishes the correspondence between the assembler instructions and the machine instructions in order to produce a program that can be executed in machine language is also called assembler.
Related terms: COBOL, FORTRAN, Programing Language, Software, PL/1, Utilization System.

**Automated Production**     See Production Process

**Automation**     This term is at present used as a noun to designate the science that deals with the study and construction of mechanisms and systems capable of fulfilling certain functions regularly and without human intervention.
Related terms: Automated Production, Office Procedures, Data Processing, Production Process, Robotics.

**Batch Processing**     A utilization technique according to which a certain number of activities—including the programs to be executed and the data related to them—are grouped into batches. The latter are introduced one after the other and are processed in a single passage through the computer, during which the user cannot modify either the sequence or the conditions of utilization.
Related terms: Utilization system, Shared Time, Real Time.

**Bit**     Several definitions apply to this term:
1. The selected unit in a binary system (for example, 0 and 1, or in logic yes and no).

2. A component element of a datum, which may represent either one of two values or states.
3. Location of a binary datum within an information unit (for example, bit no. 5 in a 16-bit memory cell).
Related terms: Bit-Second, Optical Fiber, Digital Transmission, Radio Channels.
References used: AFNOR and ISO standards, IBM dictionary.

**Bit-Second**

In a transmission mode, the number of binary signals transmitted each second.
Related terms: Bit, Digital Transmission.

**Circuit Switching**

In its simplest form, a data transmission network is composed of lines whose interconnection layout is determined in advance.

In circuit switching, the routing is reexamined at each connecting point in the network, which, depending on the load on the lines and their expected availability, itself determines the best path between the transmitter and the addressee and makes the necessary interconnections.
Related terms: Switch, Message Switching, Packet Switching.

**COBOL**

A synthetic programing language whose name is an abbreviation of Common Business-Oriented Language, developed for universal use in business applications.
Related terms: FORTRAN, Machine Language, Programing Language, PL/1, Software.

**Collective Antenna**

An aerial circuit, or antenna that makes it possible to receive communications signals and distribute

them inside a building to a number of users.
Related term: Community Antenna.

**Community Antenna**     An aerial circuit, or antenna, that makes it possible
to receive communications signals and distribute
them to a number of users located within a geographic area that may include one section of a city or
a town and its surroundings. Its main difference
from the collective antenna is its wider geographic
coverage. For this reason, community antennas require the use of more sophisticated techniques.

**Compatibility**     The term compatibility covers two complementary
concepts: on the one hand the possibility of con-
necting different computer systems and on the
other hand the capacity of different computer systems to process the same applications.

Advances in data processing and competition
among manufacturers lead to differences between
one generation of hardware and software and the
next. In order to maintain customer loyalty, each
manufacturer guarantees a certain compatibility in
its own hardware. The aim is to ensure that users
of the old systems will move to the new systems,
that users of small systems will move to more
powerful systems, and not vice versa.

The development of networks complicates this
problem: the interconnection of various computer
systems involves successive generations of hardware and software and therefore different levels
of compatibility—connection procedures and
access procedures, operation of terminals, and, finally, network-utilization languages.

Once compatibility is assured, it is possible to
change certain elements in the network without
modifying the other elements and without reducing the reliability and performance of the system.

**Components**

An element or unit that consititutes a part of a system.

In the electronics industry, the term *component* designates an elementary part that can be interconnected and contains an electronic device such as a resistor, capacitor, electron tube, transistor, integrated circuit, and so on.

Electronic components mainly include the passive components (connector, resistor, capacitor, etc.) and the active components, which perform amplification functions (tubes, transistors, integrated circuits, etc.).

At the present time, the most important electronic components are the integrated circuits, which constitute complex functional units, grouping a great number of transistor circuits on a single chip.

Related terms: Integrated Circuits, Microprocessors, Discrete Transistor.

**Connection Procedure**

In a network or a circuit, the connection between two elements is accomplished by exchanging a set of conventions in the form of a dialogue, which allows the link to be made.

Related terms: Access Procedure, Networks.

**Data Bank**

A comprehensive, nonredundant, and structured set of data, reliable and coherent, organized independently of their application, readily accessible, easily utilized, and meeting standards of confidentiality.

**Examples of data banks:**

ENEIDE   Economic and industrial data bank
DEMAIR   Air-travel information
ESCULAPE   Processing of medical histories
SYGESCO   School administration

| | |
|---|---|
| **Examples of data bank software:** | IDS   (Honeywell)<br>IMS/VS-DLI   (IBM)<br>SOCRATE   (CII)<br>MIISTIIT   (Gamma)<br>Related term: Software. |

**Digital Transmission**

Transmission of signals in which the data are transmitted in succession. Each one of them can only assume a finite number of discontinuous values.

Most often binary signals are used. In this case each datum is previously coded in the binary system.

Related terms: Modem, Networks, Analog Transmission.

**Discrete Transistor**

A transistor is an electronic device that makes use of the properties of semiconductors (silicon, germanium) and, thanks to externally connected electrodes, makes it possible to amplify an electric current.

A "discrete transistor," in contrast to an "integrated circuit," is an electronic component containing only a single transistorized device.

Related terms: Integrated Circuits, Components.

**FORTRAN**

A programming language whose name is the abbreviation of FORmulation TRANsposed, particularly suitable for the processing of scientific applications.

The relatively advanced standardization of this language facilitates portability of programs. It is used more and more to produce software for the management of computer resources and the control of operations.

Related terms: COBOL, Machine Language, Programing Language, Software, PL/1, Portability.

**Integrated Circuit**          A miniaturized electronic component embedded in
a single piece of material, grouping a set of elemen-
tary electronic devices, such as resistors, transistors,
capacitors, and so on, interconnected according to
a specific pattern.

The most recent integrated circuits used in data
processing contain on a single silicon chip hundreds
of very high-speed logic elements or tens of thousands of low-speed logic elements (LSI high-level
integration circuits).

Each one of those integrated circuits can provide
complex logical functions like adders, serial or
parallel access registers, and memories with several
thousand bits.

Generally, they form coherent families, mar-
keted by one or more component manufacturers,
whose assembly makes possible the production of
stored-up or transmission elements as well as specific software ("Firmware").

In certain cases, it may be desirable to have integrated circuits "made to order," that is, according
to a given diagram, in order to provide a complex
function more economically.

Related terms: Components, Microprocessors, Discrete Transistor.

**Intelligent Terminal**        A terminal or terminal station containing input,
output, and processing units. It allows exchanges
to be conducted with a central computer, as well
as providing for the decentralization of certain
tasks.

Generally, an intelligent terminal includes in a
single console a microcomputer, a visual display
screen, an alphanumeric keyboard, and a transmission modem to the central computer.

This master console can be tied by simple connections over short distances to further "slave"

consoles, which are not themselves equipped with microcomputers but make it possible to multiply work stations.
Related terms: Terminal, Central Unit, Input-Output Unit.

**Machine Language**

Every computer has a set of instructions expressed by means of one or more machine words.

A program consists of a suitable juxtaposition of those commands, which describe the required actions and cause them to be performed in succession.

Generally speaking, a machine instruction gives the type of the command and the memory location of the necessary parameters and codes relative to specific registers. Such elements are defined digitally, generally in binary, or using systems based on eight digits, sixteen digits, and so on.

At the time of its execution, a program is always expressed in machine language.
Related terms: Assembler, Programing Language.

**Mechanical Data Processing**

In the evolution of automated information processing, mechanical data processing corresponds to the technological stage that preceded data processing proper.

The hardware, whose technology was largely based on mechanical and electric components, was strictly specialized in the execution of categories of functions (such as sorting, classifying, reproduction, arithmetical calculations, printing, etc.) and only used punched cards or tapes as input support.

**Message Switching**

A technique consisting in receiving a message at a connecting point in a network, storing it until the appropriate output circuit is clear, and then re-transmitting it.

In this transmission technique, the message is not segmented and circulates through the network in its initial, integral form.
Related terms: Circuit Switching, Packet Switching.

**Microcomputers**

Integrated circuits and microprocessors appeared a few years ago. They tend to be used in large numbers in the most diverse hardware in the same way as simple components.

They make possible the production of microcomputers, generally in the form of one or more printed circuit cards.

Such microcomputers, which are beginning to be equipped with small peripheral systems and software, may have very numerous applications (machinery, automobiles, electric appliances, photography, miscellaneous switches, etc.). Micro-information processing therefore constitutes a potentially immense field.

**Microprocessor**

A microprocessor consists of an integrated circuit that makes up the central unit of microcomputer. It may be used directly for that purpose, or it may be used to perform other functions.
Examples of uses:
Switching units in networks
Peripheral connection units in large computers
Logical and arithmetical units of intelligent terminals
Pocket calculators
Related terms: Integrated Circuits, Components, Central Unit.

**Minicomputers**

"Minicomputers" appeared at the beginning of the sixties. Initially composed of a miniaturized central unit of relatively simple structure, this hardware was equipped with a limited software and basically was aimed at the fields of instrumentation, process control, scientific calculations at research agencies, military systems, and so on.

Since the end of the sixties, minicomputers have developed considerably as a result of decreasing costs and the extreme miniaturization of their components, as well as the considerable development of software. They are now equipped with various peripheral systems and with software enabling them to cover a much wider market; they extend over a very wide range, in which the highest performing models may rival (in terms of price performance) the most powerful computers.

The processing of information by means of minicomputers is sometimes referred to us as mini information processing.

**Modem**

A word formed with the first three letters of the two words "MOdulator" and "DEModulator." It designates a device that transforms binary signals upon transmission into signals adapted to the transmission channel (modulation function) and puts them into a form adapted to the processing component upon reception (demodulation function).

In the networks, modems provide connections between computers and transmission lines by performing the necessary code transformations and synchronizations.

Related term: Networks.

**Networks**

Initially, the concept of network designated all the circuits connecting different terminal stations.

Now this concept tends to cover a wider range; that is, it includes not only the transmission lines but also the hardware, located at the various inter-

connections and essentially charged with transmission functions, as well as the terminal stations.

The structure of networks has also undergone an
evolution. At the beginning, networks were either
hierarchically arranged (where several terminals
were connected to a single interconnection and
several interconnections to a central station), or
they were networks in which the terminal stations
were installed in succession along a loop line.

Present network structures take every possible
form, particularly one in which there are several
routes between each transmitter and each receiver.
Related terms: System Architecture, Modem, Real
Time, Terminal, Intelligent Terminal, Transmic,
Digital Transmission.

**Office Procedures**

With data-processing and audiovisual techniques,
the traditional working methods in offices are
bound to undergo profound changes. Within this
context, the term *office procedures* designates all
the techniques and processes aiming at having all
or part of the office duties performed by hardware.

The term *office procedures* therefore covers text,
image, and word-processing equipment and involves
diverse telecommunications systems.

It aims at a more effective management of documents and makes it possible to envisage the eventual development of the "paperless" office.
Related term: Telecopier.

**Optical Fibers**

Flexible wires of small diameter, consisting of a
transparent core surrounded by a frame having a
different optical index. A light beam, suitably
modulated at its source, propagates by reflection
inside the fiber.

Specifically, this new technique makes it possible to conduct very high-speed, high-capacity trans-

missions, very little affected by external interference and quite suitable for transmission over limited geographic areas.

Examples:
Data transmission: At Lannion, CNET provides a digital connection at a speed of two million bits per second, planned to reach 8.4 million bits per second.

Television: In Manhattan, a connection of several hundred meters reproduces images inside a building.

Telephone: Bell Telephone Laboratories transmits up to 50,000 simultaneous telephone conversations over a bundle of 144 optical fibers with a diameter of a half-inch (1.27 cm).
Related term: Radio Channels.

**Packet Switching**

Packet switching is a transmission method in which the messages containing the data are segmented into "packets" of fixed or varying length.

The transmission of a message requires that each one of the packets into which it is divided be accompanied by additional information capable of indicating the addresses of the transmitter and the addressee, and the nature of the required functions, as well as providing control.

Each interconnection in the network controls the quality of each packet received.

The routing method may be either fixed or flexible.

At the receiving station, the set of packets must be checked and if necessary rearranged in conformity with the transmission.

Examples of networks using packet switching: Arpa, Cyclades, Telenet, Transpac.

Related terms: Circuit Switching, Message Switching.

**Paracomputer Equipment**

This term was initially introduced to designate a group of French industrialists producing minicomputers and terminals.

In a broader sense, it is sometimes used to designate an area whose boundaries are not precisely defined: mini data-processing industries and equipment, terminals, and generally all the auxiliary equipment used around a computer, either connected or operated independently.
Related terms: Microcomputer, Minicomputer.

**PL/1**

A synthetic programing language, at the present time in very limited use. It constitutes the best-known commercial example of an attempt to group the common features of the languages used for management and those used in science.
Related terms: Assembler, COBOL, FORTRAN, Programing Language.

**Portability**

Programs are portable if different data-processing systems can execute them without modifying the application software and the data.

Thus portability is an attempt to increase the user's independence, by offering the possibility of changing the hardware while preserving the investment in application software and of using other data-processing installations in case of breakdown.

Portability occurs at several levels:
1. the language in which the applications are written, to allow the transfer of programs from one compiling device to a different one;
2. files on magnetic tape and magnetic discs, in which the writing, the coding, and the organization often differ from one manufacturer to another;

3. the structure of management software and data bases; and

4. the control language, which defines the software, the files, and the resources (such as memory size) to be used for a given application. The control language is very closely linked to the utilization system and therefore to the specificity of each data-processing system.

Related term: Compatibility.

**Production Process**

Orderly set of operations that contribute to the manufacture of a product. Production processes are either continuous (for example, the production of paper) or discontinuous (for example, the production of machinery and automobiles).

Computers are increasingly being used in the production processes to optimize manufacturing or to automate it.

Related term: Automated Production.

**Programing Language**

A programing language consists of all the actions that may be performed when a program is executed.

Most important, it contains arithmetical instructions and logic instructions. The arithmetical instructions can be executed. The purpose of the logic instructions is to modify the sequence of instructions either systematically or conditionally—for example, in terms of previous data or results.

It also contains instructions providing for the transmission of information from the input (data) to the output (printed text, diagrams, visual displays, etc.).

The program may be expressed either in the machine language applicable to the computer being used, in an assembler language, or finally in

a developed language such as FORTRAN or
COBOL. All the languages except machine language make use of a translater or compiler to
assure a match between its instructions and those
of the machine language.
Related terms: Assembler, COBOL, FORTRAN,
Machine Language, PL/1.

**Real Time**

"Real time" is the processing method that makes
it possible to receive data at any time and obtain
the results immediately. This concept originated in
connection with physical phenomena that required
the immediate processing and inclusion of results.
It has been gradually extended to all processes that
demand a very quick response.

The reaction time varies as a function of processing constraints as well as of need. Thus, in physical
systems, the immediate response corresponds to a
few milliseconds or is less than one second, while
in interrogating data banks there may be a delay of
several seconds, several minutes, or even more.
Related terms: Utilization System, Shared Time,
Batch Processing.

**Real-Time Networks**

A real-time network consists of a terminal subsystem, a transmission network, and a processing
subsystem, operating in such manner as to enable
a certain number of users to have access to it
simultaneously, with each of their requests being
fulfilled within a given time and at given intervals.
Examples of applications:
Air or train ticket reservation systems: a few
seconds' delay.
Order-taking systems: a few seconds' delay.
Payroll transmission system: the delay may reach a
few hours, at weekly or monthly intervals.
Related term: Networks.

**Remote Data Processing**     All the data-processing and telecommunications techniques that make it possible for computerized installations to exchange information.
Related term: Networks.

**Robotics**     All the research and techniques aiming at designing systems—which may or may not include software and hardware—capable of replacing man in his motor, sensory, and intellectual functions, and operating either in a predetermined fashion or by a learning process.
Related term: Automation.

**Sequential Access**     A method of retrieval or arrangement of information in a memory requiring a search from the beginning until the segment concerned or the data sought is located.

Magnetic tapes are a specific example of this mode of access.

In recording on magnetic discs, several modes of access are possible, including sequential access and other modes of access in which the location of the information is known and a systematic search of the memory is not required.

**Shared Time**     Method of processing information in which several users perform independent work on the same computer. Time periods are assigned to each user. The latter, however, may follow his own work pattern, because the reaction time is such that he can act as if the entire system were under his own permanent and exclusive control.

Access by the user may or may not be through a transmission network.
Related terms: Utilization System, Real Time, Batch Processing.

**Software**                The entire set of programs, procedures, rules, and
                            eventually documents related to the operation of
                            data-processing system.
                            Thanks to the evolution of the technology of
                            components and integrated circuits, certain com-
                            plex functions of the program are being increas-
                            ingly integrated into the hardware.
                            Related terms: Assembler, Integrated Circuit,
                            FORTRAN, Programing Language, Access Pro-
                            cedure, Utilization System.

**Switch**                  A switch is a device capable of making or breaking
                            one or more connections in a circuit, and specifi-
                            cally in a data transmission network, before the be-
                            ginning of a transmission.
                            The switch may be operated in several ways:
                            manually, electrically, electronically, or increas-
                            ingly by a microcomputer located at the connect-
                            ing points of a network.
                            Related terms: Circuit Switching, Message Switch-
                            ing, Packet Switching.

**System Architecture**     This term, initially used by computer designers, is
                            now used to designate the structure of a more or
                            less complex data-processing system, which may
                            contain one or more central units, telecommunica-
                            tions installations, and terminal stations that may
                            be interconnected, all within a geographically dis-
                            persed network.
                            Related term: Networks.

**Telecopier**              A device that makes possible the remote graphic
                            reproduction of an image (written text, diagram,
                            photograph, etc.).
                            A telecopier installation includes a transmitter, a
                            transmission system, and a receiver. At the trans-
                            mitter, the image to be transmitted is scanned by

an optical device. In the receiver, an image similar
to the original image is produced on photosensitive
or electrosensitive paper by means of another
scanning device.

The transmission uses either analog signals (short-
distance connections) or digital signals.

Telecopying often makes use of the standard
telephone network.
Related term: Office Procedures.

**Terminal**

Input and/or output station connected to a com-
puter by any data transmission and allowing the
transmission and/or reception of messages.
Examples:
Dialogue terminal
Graphic terminal
Related terms: Intelligent Terminal, Central Unit,
Input-Output Unit.

**TRANSMIC**

Information transmission service by modulation of
coded impulses (MIC—*M*odulation d'*I*mpulsions
*C*odées) envisaged by PTT and intended to supple-
ment Transpac for very large volume transmissions.
Related terms: Networks, Digital Transmission.

**Unbundling**

A marketing method for computers used by some
manufacturers and consisting in preparing separate
invoices for the computer as such, regarded as hardware, and for the software that allows its use.

Generally, unbundling is used for application
software. Some manufacturers are also beginning
to use it for basic software (utilization systems,
compilers, etc.).

**Utilization System**

The utilization system includes all the basic software that makes it possible to execute the various
tasks assigned to a data-processing system.

Specifically, it performs the role of arranging the sequence of work, optimizing the use of the internal resources of the computer and automatically managing input and output.

Furthermore, the utilization system enables several users to work simultaneously without being aware of each other. Thus it assures a continuous monitoring of the flow of work and its progress.

While it offers numerous advantages, the utilization system itself is a set of programs that occupy part of the resources of the data processing system, thereby reducing its performance.

Related terms: Shared Time, Real Time, Batch Processing.

# NOTES

1. This neologism closely resembles the term used in the United States, "compunication." The fact that the American term stresses the computer and ours the telecommunications aspect is not accidental. It expresses a set of power relationships that in France give the upper hand to the latter.

**Chapter 2**

1. See supporting document no. 1, "The Computer at the Crossroads."

2. See appendix 2, "Data Banks."

3. See glossary, "digital transmission."

4. See appendix 1, "Network Systems, Telecommunications, and Telematics."

5. See ibid. and supporting document no. 10, "Advanced Application of Computerization," monograph no. 1.

6. See appendix 1, "Network Systems, Telecommunications, and Telematics."

7. See supporting document no. 10, "Advanced Applications of Computerization," monograph no. 10.

8. See appendix 1, "Network Systems, Telecommunications, and Telematics."

9. See ibid. and glossary.

10. Ibid.

11. As we shall see, political considerations may require protocols that transcend exclusively technical needs.

12. See appendix 2, "Data Banks."

**Chapter 3**

1. Their disaggregation is too weak for analysis of phenomena visible only in the smallest sector of the economy. The short-term models (the STAR model, the 600-branch input-output table) do not incorporate technological advances; the medium-term models define technological progress as an exogenous variable; and there is no long-term model. In any case, any long-term model would be faced with the difficulty of linking "pointed" technological effects with radical changes in the indexes of production and consumption, the only means of arriving at the laws governing behavior in a transformed society. France is behind in this type of projection, but its limits are obvious, even in those countries that have devoted the most effort to it. Appendix 4 stresses the risky, unsatisfactory nature of the considerable research that has been done on this subject, especially in the United States and Japan.

2. See appendix 3, "Data Processing and Macroeconomics."

3. See appendix 5, "An Approach to an Economic Evaluation of the Uses of Data Processing."

4. This examination is based on single studies of large enterprises in the tertiary sector, but their cooperation was so active that only aggregate results on productivity and employment will be published.

5. See appendix 10, "Data Processing and French Government Administration," additional note 1 on Social Security.

6. This figure of 800,000 employees refers to secretaries in the strict sense of the term, rather than to all office workers, who number two million.

7. See supporting document no. 10, "Advanced Applications of Computerization," monograph no. 4.

8. As with the service sector, the following statements are based on an examination of large French enterprises.

9. See supporting document no. 10, "Advanced Applications of Computerization," monograph no. 6.

10. Which refers to protection-related services as well as production itself.

11. See the glossary under "Robotics" and supporting document no. 10, "Advanced Applications of Computerization," monograph no. 6.

12. The threshold effect is an extremely complex factor. The quality of the sales network, maintenance guarantees, and traditional customer relationships also enter into a choice in which price plays a predominant but not an exclusive role.

13. Thus it seems, on the basis of a variant of the DMS model constructed to deal with this point (see appendix 3, "Data Processing and Macroeconomics," supplementary note 3), that a 10 percent productivity increase in the services rendered to such enterprises leads over three years to a slight improvement in the level of exports. However, this in itself does not lead to an improvement in the trade balance, because any increase in investment, which is related in this case to a surplus of autofinancing, is inevitably accompanied by an excess of imports, given the current structure of French foreign trade. However, this phenomenon is not juggled away as a result of that: productivity gains in the service sector stimulate exports.

Still, in order to be fully effective, exports must be strong enough to enable French industry to overcome its competitive handicap. Otherwise perverse effects—job losses—are introduced without any increase in export markets.

14. See the GEPI (International Prospects Study Group) study, "Worldwide Growth and Strategies of Specialization."

15. See the GEPI study, "An Economy in Search of Optimal Specialization: Japan."

16. These phenomena are analyzed in appendix 3, "Data Processing and Macroeconomics."

17. . . . and even then nothing guarantees that the new outlets would make it possible to create jobs in numbers equal to or larger than the number of places abolished during the period of rationalization. In order to resolve this issue, one would have to be able to measure the "job content" of various types of exports, which cannot be done under the French statistical setup. Without pertinent figures, two concepts oppose each other. One of them, which is less evident, and which assures the evolution of exports toward products in which the value added contains an increasingly larger proportion of wages, would lead to the conclusion that foreign trade represents an increasing volume of employment. The other, which is more likely, and which is based on the notion of an international division of labor in which the industrialized countries specialize in the most developed sectors, which are consequently the most automated, leads to the fear that total employment related to exports will tend to decrease even if exports increase. Only an exhaustive study would make it possible to disprove or confirm one or the other of these lines of reasoning.

18. Forecast models do not make it possible to measure the consequences of a gradual shift of the demand toward collective services and toward new types of goods. However, they offer the opportunity to take note of their economic effect. A variant of the DMS model (see appendix 3, "Data Processing and Macroeconomics") based on a transfer of household demand toward the tertiary sector, even the most traditional segments (transportation, telecommunications, services), shows a relative improvement of employment, to be sure at the cost of accelerated inflation.

19. See appendix 7, "The Data-Processing Industry (Its

Development, Its Policies, and Its Situation in Various Countries)."

20. See appendix 4, "The Information Society and New Growth: A Study of Some Foreign Approaches (Japan, American Research)."

21. List of major projects of the Jacudi plan, appendix 4.

22. The first industrial option extending the "current trend"; the second is a social option in which everybody is provided with maximum benefits in matters of health, education, housing, insurance, and so on—this option would suffer from inflation in terms of financing collective facilities; the third is a "leisure" or hedonist option, in which amusements, trips, vacations, and so on are developed—it would cause congestion and debase the quality of life.

23. See the critique in appendix 4.

**Chapter 4**

1. Taken in their legal signification, the terms deconcentration, decentralization, and autonomy offer a better representation of the possible forms of organization than the professional vocabulary—distributed computerization, microcomputerization, minicomputerization—which provides a vehicle for conflicts of interest.

2. See "Report on Operating Conditions in the Distribution of Fresh Food Products," by Inspectors of Finance Eveno, Hannoun, Lamy, and Minc.

3. See supporting document no. 6; Data Processing and Local Power."

4. This problem is treated in supporting document no. 4, which deals in more general terms with the total effect of computer technology on medicine.

5. See supporting document no. 7, dealing with working conditions.

6. The CFDT has enriched this debate; see "The Ravages of Progress," published by Seuil in July 1977.

7. The legal problems relating to computerization are reviewed in supporting document no. 5.

8. This question, which was not dealt with in this report, deserves special examination; see bibliography in appendix 12.

**Chapter 5**

1. Cf. appendix 7, "The Data-Processing Industry."

2. IBM France contributes in a major way to French data-processing exports.

3. After some attempts that ran up against antitrust regulations, IBM managed to obtain this authorization by presenting itself as a minority partner in a company—COMSAT—whose majority shareholders are institutional investors, apparently in the role of sleeping partners.

4. This prediction, agrees with the type of analysis sketched out by Brzezinski in *The Technetronic Revolution* (Calmann-Lévy, 1971).

5. IBM headquarters in the United States.

6. This section deals with the policy aspects of standardization. Its technical aspects are analyzed in the following chapter, "Telecommunications."

7. Cf. appendix 1, "Network Systems, Telecommunications, and Telematics."

8. Ibid.

9. Cf. appendix 2, "Data Banks."

10. Ibid.

**Chapter 6**

1. Cf. appendix 1, "Network Systems, Telecommunications, and Telematics."

2. Thus it is that TDF states that it is impossible for a direct television satellite to provide data transmission, in this way justifying the need to have a satellite of its own. On the other hand, the DGT feels that the future lies in mixed satellites associating telephone traffic, data transmission, and television. It thus hopes to relocate within its own sphere radio and television broadcasting. As for the CNES, it seems to support the technical position of TDF, running up against what experts for IBM have asserted to us.

Likewise, the organizations diverge on the eventual possibility of broadcasting to the satellite from modest-sized individual antenna. The DGT has asserted that interference between broadcasting antennas will be substantial enough to prevent individual broadcasts and that it will be necessary to employ large collective antennas. This is not without its consequences: in the first case—simple individual broadcast—the government monopoly is outflanked, technically speaking; in the second—no possibility of individual boradcasts—the technological constraints opportunely reinforce the legal basis of the monopoly. On this point, the CNES, which could not benefit finan-

cially from the preservation of the monopoly, has contra-
dicted the DGT: it feels that small, individual, neighbor-
ing antennas will without difficulty be able to broadcast
to the satellite. The same option is shared by the IBM
experts, who believe that such broadcasts are possible.

It is not within the scope of the present report to settle
these quarrels. But if it seems paradoxical to see such
strong divergences expressed on very precise points, it is
even more troubling to consider how much these opinions
correspond to the institutional interests of the organizations expressing them.

3. Cf. appendix 1, "Network Systems, Telecommunications, and Telematics,"

4. Ibid.

5. Transpac is a public network designed to transmit
computerized correspondence and various types of messages. Subscribers have access either directly or by telephone, allowing many users to obtain at relatively low
cost services that previously required renting special
telephone lines.

6. This report was the occasion for the Public Accounting
Office and the DGT to reconcile their viewpoints and
avoid bothersome duplication.

7. Cf. appendix 1, "Network Systems, Telecommunications, and Telematics," and supporting document no. 10,
"Advanced Applications of Computerization," monograph no. 10.

8. In fact, Transpac does not guarantee complete interconnectability. The X 25 protocol, which the DGT succeeded in having adopted by international interests, constitutes a major stage, obliging the systems architects* to
unify part of their internal software.* It nevertheless
remains fairly distant from the "virtual equipment" protocol, the only technical procedure that allows any terminal to converse with any other. Yet this first level of
dissemination imposes technical and financial constraints.
The manufacturers do not give in without resistance:
their objective is less to adapt to X 25 than to conform to
it by modifying their systems as little as possible. Thus
IBM succeeded in protecting its SNA system by a "black
box" that allows it to follow X 25 without disturbing its
software. This leads one to imagine that the manufacturers
are preserving their systems in the expectation of better
days when they will be able to set up their communications in perfect freedom thanks to satellites, assuming
they function as simple reflectors.

9. Cf. appendix 1, "Network Systems, Telecommunications, and Telematics."

10. The Institute of Economic and Social Research on Telecommunications (IREST), the Institute of Socioeconomic Research and Information (IRIS) of the University of Paris–Dauphine, the Institute for Data-Processing and Automation Research (IRIA) for certain aspects, as well as researchers scattered throughout academic institutions, devote part or all of their activity to this subject.

**Chapter 7**

1. Cf. appendix 9, "Service and Data-Processing Consulting Companies."

2. Cf. appendix 12, "Intermediate and Small Users."

3. Cf. appendix 5, "An Approach to an Economic Evaluation of the Uses of Data Processing."

4. Ibid.

5. Cf. supporting document no. 8, "Information Research and Technology."

**Chapter 8**

1. See appendix 10, "Data Processing and French Government Administration."

2. See ibid., supplementary note 3, "Data Processing in the Direction Générale des Impôts."

3. See ibid., supplementary note 1, "Data Processing in Social Security."

4. See ibid., general note.

5. Rationalisation des choix budgétaires (rationalization of budgetary choices).

6. Among whom some might not or should not be officials (private managers, French or foreign academics).

7. In order to solve the delicate questions of administrative jurisdictions and prerogatives, the committee would include the ministers concerned in addition to the prime minister, the minister of economy and finance, and the state secretary for public functions, who would be its permanent members.

8. See supporting document no. 6, "Data Processing and Local Power."

9. With respect to really vital secrets, present techniques make it possible to protect them without difficulty. The

annoyance of data processing can most often be remedied by better applications, also involving data processing.

**Chapter 9**

1. In the United States in 1900, farmworkers constituted 35 percent of the total active population, in contrast with the present 4 percent. The industrial labor force peaked in 1950 at the level of 40 percent. The population employed in the "information sector," one-half of that in the industrial sector in 1940, is now twice as large. (See appendix 4.) Certainly, this classification is debatable (see ibid.), but it points out an important phenomenon. In France, subject to the same reservations, 45 percent of the active population is already working in the information sector.

Cf. L. Ferrandon and J.G. de Chalvron, *Poids relatif de l'information dans l'ensemble des activités économiques*, published by the Ecole Nationale Supérieure des Télécommunications, November 1976.

2. See, for example, the west coast of the United States, Canada, and Italy.

3. Since then, Small Is Beautiful has become a slogan in the United States.

4. These trends are already appearing; see chapter 6.

5. This report cannot analyze the development and the future of the various conflicts "outside production." Language and knowledge have been considered both because they are at the focal point of all other conflicts and because in the long run they may be directly affected by telematics.

**Chapter 10**

1. Either one remains within a philosophy of uncertainty, or one clings to poor laws with a univocal and fixed determination. . . . The pluralist in vain points out to the dialectician the poverty of his structures and the constantly repeated error of his perspective" (Michel Serres, Hermès 1).

2. By contrast, a monotonous flow of facts and events can be the most formidable tool of disinformation.

"In our societies, the overabundance of signs matches the poverty of meaning" (François Bott).